Punch Needle
Friends

Punch Needle Friends

20 ADORABLE PROJECTS TO EMBROIDER

FAUSTINE DUWICQUET WITH CATHY DUWICQUET

Interweave

A Quarto Book

Interweave
An imprint of Penguin Random House LLC
penguinrandomhouse.com

Conceived, edited, and designed by
Quarto Publishing plc,
an imprint of the Quarto Group
The Old Brewery
6 Blundell Street
London N7 9BH

QUAR.340569

Printed in China

10 9 8 7 6 5 4 3 2 1

ISBN 9780593331958

Editor: Ruth Patrick
Designer: Rachel Cross
Photographer: Holly Jolliffe
Illustrator: Kuo Kang Chen
Proofreader: Caroline West
Editorial assistant: Charlene Fernandes
Deputy art director: Martina Calvio
Art director: Gemma Wilson
Publisher: Samantha Warrington

Contents

•••••••••••••••••••••••••••••••••••

Meet Faustine!

From a young age, my mother and grandmother introduced me to creative hobbies, and my desire to learn several techniques has grown with me over the years. One day, my mum and I decided to share our creations which reflect our mother and daughter bond. We thus created our brand: De Mer en Fil.

Two years ago, the punch needle took a more central role in my creations. This technique combines both drawing and yarn; the perfect combo for me. Its ease of use allows you to clear your head and have a good time without thinking too much. I enjoy the slow, meditative flow of punch needle, and it is easy to unpick if you find you have made a mistake.

In this book, you will learn the punch needle basics through the twenty featured projects. The first project is the easiest, and each builds on the last, so by the end of the book you will have discovered the key to letting your imagination run wild in your own designs. A word of warning: punch needle is a very compelling craft and you may soon find yourself addicted!

Tools and Materials

From threading your needle to framing your project, on the following pages is a guide to the most useful tools and materials you will need.

Meet your punch needle

There are several kinds of punch needle available. They differ either by the way the yarn will be threaded into the needle (through the slit or with a copper thread), the size of the yarn that will be used (fine or thick), or by the length of the loop (short or long). Always ensure you have the correct thickness of yarn for the punch needle you are using. To make the projects in this book, you will need a needle for super bulky weight yarns (small loop) and a needle for lightweight yarns.

Punch needle for light yarns is used for yarns that are knitted with size 2–6 (3–4mm) needles and allows you to create loops of ⅛in (3mm). In the projects, this size of needle is used for eyelashes and whiskers. The punch needle shown is an Oxford no.14 regular punch needle.

Punch needle for super bulky yarns (small loop) is used for yarns that are knitted with size 10–13 (6–9mm) needles and allows you to create loops of ¼in (5mm). The punch needle shown is an Oxford no.10 regular punch needle.

Punch needle for super bulky yarns (large loop) is used for yarns that are knitted with size 10–15 (6–10mm) needles and allows you to create loops of ½in (1cm). The punch needle shown is an Oxford no.8 regular punch needle.

Punch needle with adjustable handle is used for yarns that are knitted with size 10–15 (6–10mm) needles and allows you to create loops measuring ⅛–½in (3–10mm).

Choosing yarn

The choice of yarn is important because it must both be compatible with the fabric, but also with the needle. If the diameter of the yarn is too large, the yarn will jam in the needle. If the diameter of the thread is too small, the thread is no longer retained by the weft of the fabric that has been pierced by too large a needle.

To make the projects in this book, we used super bulky yarn that is knitted with size 10–13 (6–9mm) needles. As a general guide to yarn quantities, we use approximately half a ball of yarn for the background and a total of one ball for all the facial elements, made up of different colors. For the background, we often use a double strand of finer yarn as the color palette is more varied than that of super bulky yarns. The eyelashes and whiskers are worked with light yarn that is knitted with size 2–6 (3–4mm) needles. See page 7 for information on the best punch needles to use with these yarns.

Some yarn recommendations of varying compositions, including cotton, are given on this page. Other materials are also compatible, such as trapilho, silk, jersey, or recycled fabric. As long as you can thread your needle with it, you can use it. The possibilities are endless.

1. DMC Knitty 10 This is a thick, 100-percent acrylic yarn that knits with size 15 (10mm) needles. It is ideal for punch needles for super bulky yarn or a punch needle with adjustable handle (see page 7).

2. Alison & Mae XL This yarn is made with 100-percent acrylic, and is knitted with size 10.5 (7mm) needles. It is ideal for punch needles for super bulky yarn or a punch needle with adjustable handle (see page 7).

3. Phil Rapido This yarn is made up of 5 percent acrylic, 25 percent wool, and 50 percent polyamide, and knits with size 10.5 (7mm) needles. It is ideal for punch needles for bulky yarn or a punch needle with adjustable handle (see page 7).

4. DMC Natura XL This is a 100-percent cotton ball that is knitted with size 10 (6mm) needles. It is ideal for punch needles for super bulky yarn or a punch needle with adjustable handle (see page 7).

5. Phil Looping This is an 80-percent acrylic and 20-percent wool blend that knits with size 10 (6mm) needles. This wool is rather fine for punch needle, but we find threading a double strand of yarn with a punch needle for bulky yarn works well.

Other tools and materials

CANVAS

1. Monk's cloth is a 100-percent cotton canvas, and is compatible with punch needles. It has a very wide and flexible weft, and has white borders every 2in (5cm) as a guide.

2. Floba is a blend of linen and viscose. It is a little more expensive than monk's cloth but is of very good quality because the fiber is flexible and does not break.

3. Burlap is a natural fiber canvas that is a good canvas option to start with. It is less flexible and less pleasant to work with than the previous fabrics but has the advantage of being inexpensive.

HOOPS

4. Morgan No-Slip Hoops are round plastic embroidery hoops used to keep the canvas taut. Select a diameter slightly larger than your project.

5. Wooden hoops hold the canvas taut less well but are still effective. It will just be necessary to re-stretch the canvas more often.

6. Bamboo hoops are more flexible and used as decorative hoops because they don't hold the stretched canvas taut enough for stitching. The diameter of the hoop must be smaller than the embroidery hoop.

Plastic frames are made of tubes and clips, and are convenient to use for square projects.

SCISSORS

Universal for paper cutting.
Sewing to cut the canvases.
7. Embroidery to cut the threads and loops.
8. Appliqué to cut the loops.

PENS

9. Erasable pen is used to draw the circle around the head. The lines cannot be seen at the edges of the final project as the ink disappears within a few hours.

10. Marker pen is used to reproduce the drawing on the fabric to make the lines stand out.

Punch Needle Techniques

On these pages you will find the techniques to help you to create the projects featured in the book, from reproducing the design on your canvas to framing your finished creation in a decorative hoop. Instructions for the iron-on transfers can be found on pages 118–119.

TRANSFERRING THE DESIGN TO THE CANVAS

 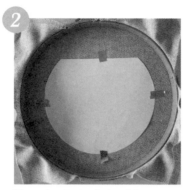 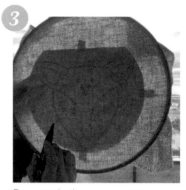

Enlarge your chosen design from the templates section (see pages 118–127) by 50 percent on a photocopier and cut the sheet of paper to the dimensions of the decorative hoop.

Place the design behind the embroidery hoop, securing it with repositionable adhesive tape.

Position the hoop against a window so it is lit from behind and copy the drawing with a marker.

TRANSFERRING THE DESIGN TO THE REVERSE OF THE CANVAS

Most of the projects in the book have facial elements that need to be worked on the back of the canvas, which are shown on a diagram at the beginning of each project. The method below also applies if you are working a project with an iron-on transfer (see instructions on pages 118–119).

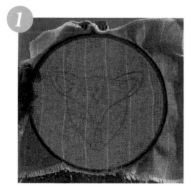 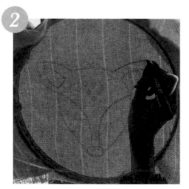 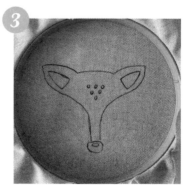

Turn the hoop over so the back of the canvas is facing you. Position the hoop against a window so it is lit from behind.

Trace the elements to be worked on the back of the canvas as shown on the diagram at the beginning of each project.

The back of the canvas is now ready for your project.

FITTING THE CANVAS IN THE EMBROIDERY HOOP

Unscrew the hoop and divide the two parts: the inner circle and the outer circle.

Position the canvas on the inner circle of the hoop.

Add the outer part of the hoop from above.

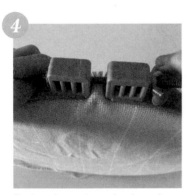

Push in the circle and tighten the screw to close the hoop.

Pull on the four corners of the canvas to stretch it well.

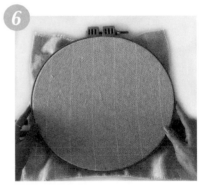

The canvas is now ready for your project.

HOW TO THREAD YOUR PUNCH NEEDLE

1: Pass the end of the thread through the eye of the needle on the slit side.

2: Hold the end of the thread and slide the taut thread through the slit.

3: Pull the end of the thread so that it is positioned in the slot.

USING THE PUNCH NEEDLE

1. Thread the yarn through the eye of the needle.

2. Insert the needle in the canvas, pushing it in as far as it will go. The slit should be pointing upward.

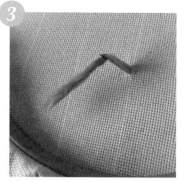

3. Gently pull the thread through to the back of the canvas, leaving a tail of around 1¼in (3cm).

4. Pull the needle out on the front side so the point touches the canvas. Replant the needle a little farther (about ¼in/5mm) to create your first flat stitch.

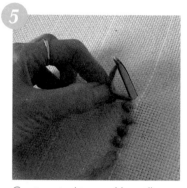

5. Continue in this way. You will see each stitch creates a loop on the other side of the canvas.

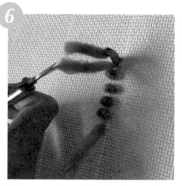

6. When you have finished, gently pull the thread to the back of the canvas and cut it, leaving a tail of around 1¼in (3cm).

PUNCHING ON THE BACK OF THE CANVAS

In the project sequences throughout the book, if the back of the canvas is shown you will see the following arrow on the step picture.

PUNCHING TIPS

To fill in an element of the design, always start by filling in the outline and working from the outside to the inside.

Make sure that the following rows are staggered from the first row to create even coverage.

When you punch in a circle, make sure that the stitches are staggered with the previous row.

When punching in a straight line, make sure the stitches are the same size.

Flat stitch as seen from the back of the canvas.

Types of stitches

Punch needle allows you to create a number of different types of stitch. There are no hard-and-fast rules—the most important thing is that each stitch is strong enough not to come undone. Below are the main stitches that will be used in this book.

1: Flat stitches are made on the front side of the canvas. They are small, neat, and flat, allowing precise filling of the design. The loops are longer on the back of the canvas.

2: Looped stitches are flat stitches made on the back side of the canvas, which creates a longer loop on the front side. We add relief and emphasis to areas of the design with these stitches.

3: Cut loops are looped stitches, which are then cut to create a fluffy, furry effect.

4: Long cut loops are looped stitches, which are then manually pulled on the front of the canvas to create a long loop. The loops are cut to create fringes and then combed lightly to create long hair or fur.

MAKING EMBELLISHMENTS

Many animals in the book are embellished with pretty felt flowers and leaves, or a bow that can be used either as a hair accessory or a bow tie. Instructions on how to make them can be found below, and when complete they can be glued to your embroidery. The embellishments templates can be found on page 127.

Bow

1 Photocopy the template (see page 127), cut it out, pin the two pieces to the felt, and cut around them.

2 Glue the two ends of the larger piece of felt by putting a dot of glue in the middle on each side.

3 Fold in half on the side opposite to the closing line and put dots of glue on the back and front.

4 Fold the top and the bottom parts together to form a concertina shape. Wrap the small piece of felt around the bow and secure with glue.

Flower

1 Photocopy the template (see page 127), cut it out, pin it to the felt, and cut around it.

2 Roll the felt, starting with the outside of the pattern (the end that will be the inside of the flower).

3 Make the underside of the flower even and flat. Glue the edges with a glue gun as you go.

4 When you have finished rolling, glue the circle end underneath.

Leaf

Photocopy the template (see page 127), cut it out, pin it to the felt, and cut around it.

FINISHING

To finish the projects, we mount them in a decorative hoop. To hide the back of the hoop nicely, we attach a piece of cotton fabric that we cut to the diameter of the decorative hoop.

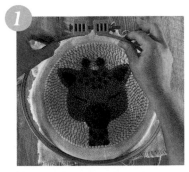

Remove the canvas from the embroidery hoop. Place the canvas on the decorative hoop (see instructions on page 11).

Stretch the canvas well so the fabric cannot be seen.

Run the glue gun around the inside edge of the hoop on the back of the canvas to fix the embroidery to the hoop.

Fold the corners of the canvas in toward the inside of the hoop and trim if necessary.

Glue a piece of cotton fabric to the back to finish.

OTHER DISPLAY IDEAS

In the instructions for each project, we have suggested using the punch needle motifs as wall hangings but they can be displayed in many other ways. Below are some ideas. Rather than gluing your project to a decorative hoop, you will need to secure the stitches with iron-on canvas applied to the back of the embroidery.

Blanket patch Trim the canvas around the embroidery, tuck the excess behind, and sew the edge securely to the blanket using a tapestry needle and yarn. This method can be used if you are attaching the design to any flat fabric, such as a **sweater**, a **child's pyjama case**, a **child's toy bag**, or an **embroidery** or **tote bag**.

Cushion Fill the outline of the design in a square shape instead of round, to the size of your pillow cover. Attach the embroidery to the pillow cover as per the blanket patch.

Hot water bottle cover Use a rectangular plastic frame to hold your canvas and extend the background of the design to the size of your hot water bottle cover. When complete, attach the embroidery to the hot water bottle cover as per the blanket patch.

Tea cozy Fill the outline of the design in a circular shape to the size of your tea cozy. When complete, attach the embroidery to the tea cozy as per the blanket patch.

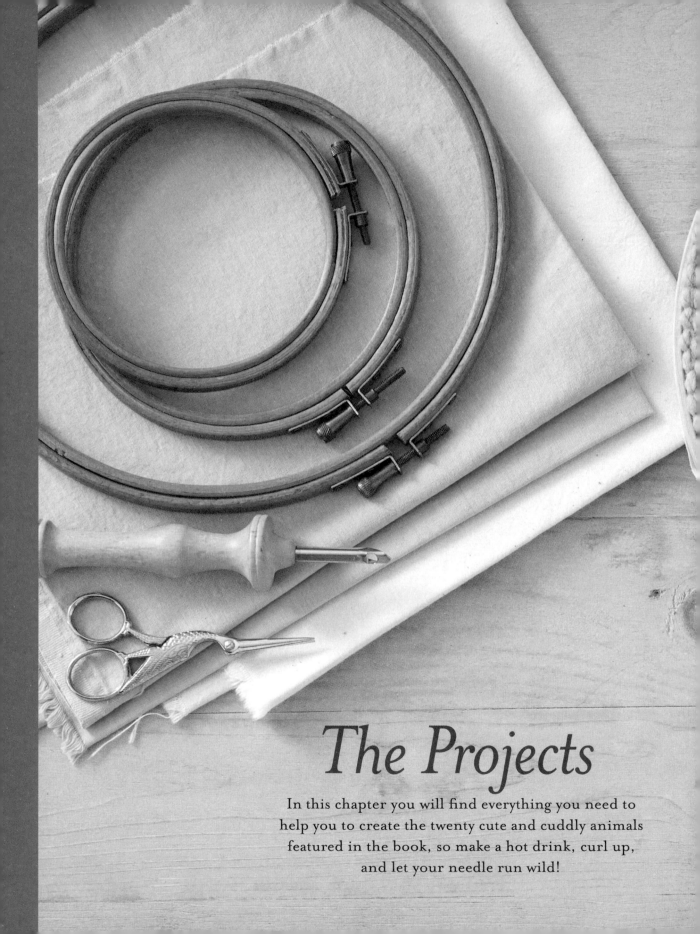

The Projects

In this chapter you will find everything you need to help you to create the twenty cute and cuddly animals featured in the book, so make a hot drink, curl up, and let your needle run wild!

Polar Bear

This cute polar bear is an ideal project to start with, since we only use one type of stitch and one side of the canvas. If you would like to work a girl polar bear, you can add flowers or make the bow tie into a hair accessory (see page 14).

TOOLS AND MATERIALS

· Monk's cloth fabric 15 x 15in (38 x 38cm)
· Non-slip embroidery hoop 12in (30cm)
· Transfer 1 from iron-on transfer sheet (see envelope at back of book)
· Punch needle for super bulky yarn
· Embroidery scissors
· Decorative wooden hoop 10½in (26cm)
· Erasable pen
· Glue gun and glue sticks
· Felt for bow (see page 14)

YARN COLORS USED

SUPER BULKY
· Black
· Gray
· White
· Blue

STITCHES USED

SEE PAGE 13 FOR STITCH GUIDE
· Flat

1

Stretch the canvas over the embroidery hoop (see page 11), then reproduce the design on the front of the canvas using the iron-on transfer sheet (see envelope at back of book). Thread the punch needle with black yarn (see page 11).

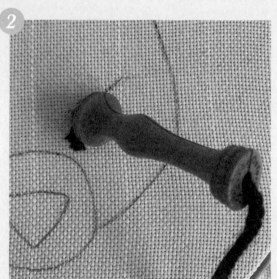

2

Insert the needle in the corner of one eye, pushing it in as far as it will go. On the back side, pull the thread through, leaving a tail of around 1¼in (3cm). Gently pull out the punch needle to the level of the canvas, then insert the punch needle again a little farther. You have your first stitch.

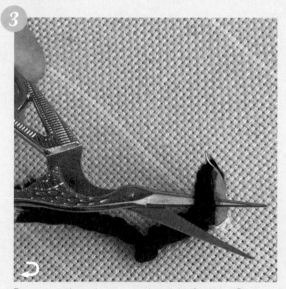

3

Repeat until you have completed the first eye. Once this is finished, leave the needle in the canvas and turn the hoop over. Carefully remove the tip of the needle and cut the thread, leaving about 1¼in (3cm). Repeat for the other eye.

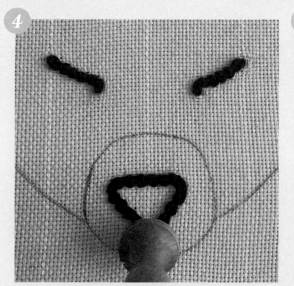

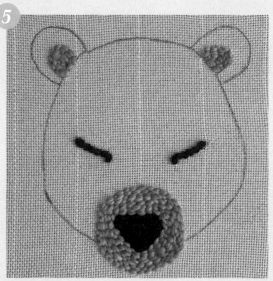

Fill in the nose, starting with the outline and then working toward the center. When the nose is complete, cut the thread on the other side of the canvas as before.

Thread the gray yarn for the muzzle and ears. Work in the same way as step 4.

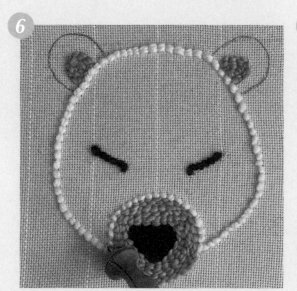

Thread the white yarn and fill in the face, starting with the outline and working from the outside to the inside. After the face is finished, fill in the ears with white. The bear's face is now finished.

Using the inner ring of the decorative hoop, draw a circle around the polar bear's head with an erasable pen. Thread the blue yarn and fill this circle, working from the outside to the inside. Remove the canvas from the embroidery hoop, then fit it on the decorative hoop (see page 15).

Rabbit

•••

This little rabbit will introduce you to three types of stitches: the flat stitch, the looped stitch, and the cut loop. We will also stitch on both sides of the canvas to give more relief to the design. We will give the rabbit a fluffy nose and add eyelashes and whiskers.

TOOLS AND MATERIALS

- Monk's cloth fabric 15 x 15in (38 x 38cm)
- Non-slip embroidery hoop 12in (30cm)
- Template 1 (see page 118)
- Marker pen
- Punch needle for super bulky yarn
- Appliqué or embroidery scissors
- Punch needle for light yarn
- Decorative wooden hoop 10½in (26cm)
- Erasable pen
- Glue gun and glue sticks
- Felt for flowers and leaves (see page 14)

YARN COLORS USED

SUPER BULKY
- Black
- Pink
- White
- Gray

LIGHT
- Black

STITCHES USED

SEE PAGE 13 FOR STITCH GUIDE
- Flat
- Looped
- Cut

WORKING IN RELIEF

The shaded areas of the diagram show the parts of the design that should be worked on the back of the canvas. This creates longer loops that may be cut to create additional texture and relief. For instructions on how to transfer the design to both sides of the canvas, see page 10.

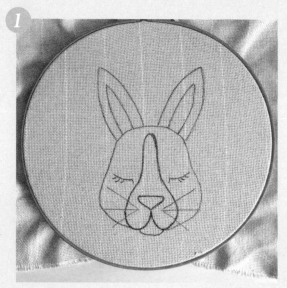

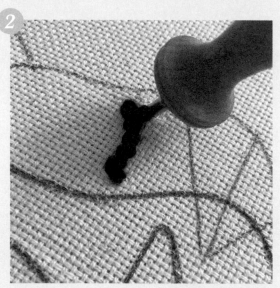

Stretch the canvas over the embroidery hoop (see page 11) and reproduce the design on the front of the canvas (see page 10). Reproduce the elements to be in relief on the back of the canvas (see page 10). Thread the punch needle with black yarn (see page 11).

Insert the needle in the corner of one eye and pull the thread through on the back, leaving a tail of around 1¼in (3cm). Work the first eye. Once finished, leave the needle in the canvas and turn the hoop over. Carefully remove the tip of the needle and cut the thread, leaving about 1¼in (3cm). Repeat for the other eye.

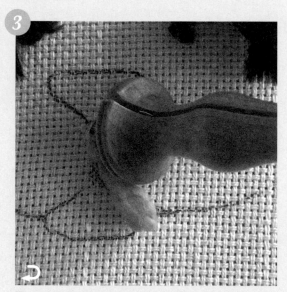

Thread the pink yarn, turn the hoop over, and fill in the nose, starting with the outline and working toward the center. When the nose is complete, cut the thread on the other side of the canvas as before.

Turn the hoop over and cut the loops with the scissors to create a fluffy effect.

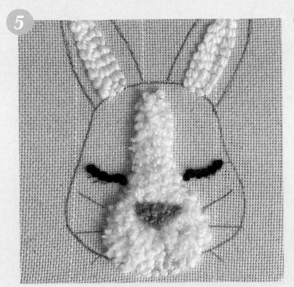

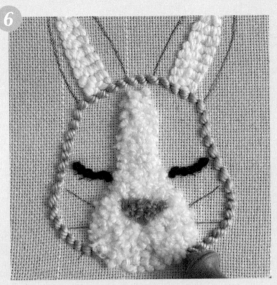

Thread the white yarn and work the middle of the face that will be in relief on the back side of the canvas, then turn the hoop over to the front side and cut the loops as for the nose. Fill the inside of the ears and the mouth on the front side.

Staying on the front side of the canvas, thread the gray yarn and fill in the remaining elements, always starting with the outlines and working from the outside to the inside.

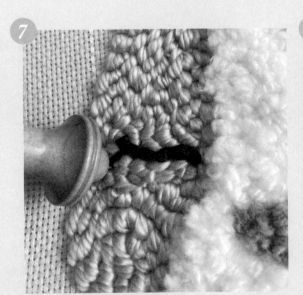

Thread the light black yarn and add the eyelashes by inserting the needle at the edge of the eye. Cut the thread on the back and do the same for the other lashes. The face of the rabbit is now finished.

Using the inner ring of the decorative hoop, draw a circle around the rabbit's head with an erasable pen. Thread the pink yarn and fill this circle, starting with the outline. Add the whiskers in the same way as the eyelashes. Remove the canvas from the embroidery hoop, then fit it on the decorative hoop (see page 15).

TRANSFER 2

Giraffe

●●

This gorgeous giraffe is worked in the colors of the savanna, and we use looped stitches to emphasize the giraffe's muzzle and horns. The flat stitches are worked on the front of the canvas and the loops are worked on the back.

TOOLS AND MATERIALS

· Monk's cloth fabric 15 x 15in (38 x 38cm)
· Non-slip embroidery hoop 12in (30cm)
· Transfer 2 from iron-on transfer sheet (see envelope at back of book)
· Marker pen
· Punch needle for super bulky yarn
· Embroidery scissors
· Decorative wooden hoop 10½in (26cm)
· Erasable pen
· Glue gun and glue sticks

YARN COLORS USED

SUPER BULKY

· Black
· Mustard
· Brown
· Ecru

STITCHES USED

SEE PAGE 13 FOR STITCH GUIDE

· Flat
· Looped

WORKING IN RELIEF

The shaded areas of the diagram show the parts of the design that should be worked on the back of the canvas. This creates longer loops that may be cut to create additional texture and relief. For instructions on how to transfer the design to the back of the canvas, see page 10.

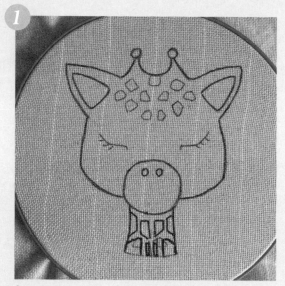

Stretch the canvas over the embroidery hoop (see page 11), then reproduce the design on the front of the canvas using the iron-on transfer sheet (see envelope at back of book). Reproduce the elements to be in relief on the back of the canvas (see page 10). Thread the punch needle with black yarn (see page 11).

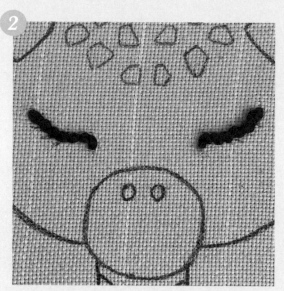

Insert the needle in the corner of one eye on the front side. On the back side, pull the thread through, leaving a tail of around 1¼in (3cm). Work both of the giraffe's eyes. We will continue on the front of the canvas and work the nostrils in black later.

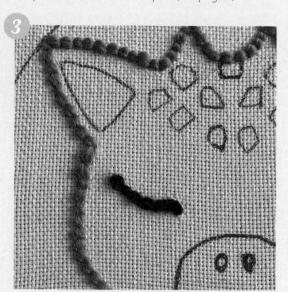

Thread the mustard yarn and start with the outline of the face, including the ears and yellow parts of the neck.

Thread the black yarn and work the nostrils (about three stitches) on the back of the canvas.

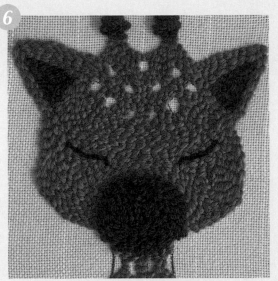

Staying on the back of the canvas, thread the brown yarn and work the muzzle and the horns.

Turn the hoop over to the front and fill the inside of the ears and all the spots in brown.

Using the inner ring of the decorative hoop, draw a circle around the giraffe's head with an erasable pen. Thread the ecru yarn and fill this circle, working from the outside to the inside. Once finished, remove the canvas from the embroidery hoop and fit it on the decorative hoop (see page 15).

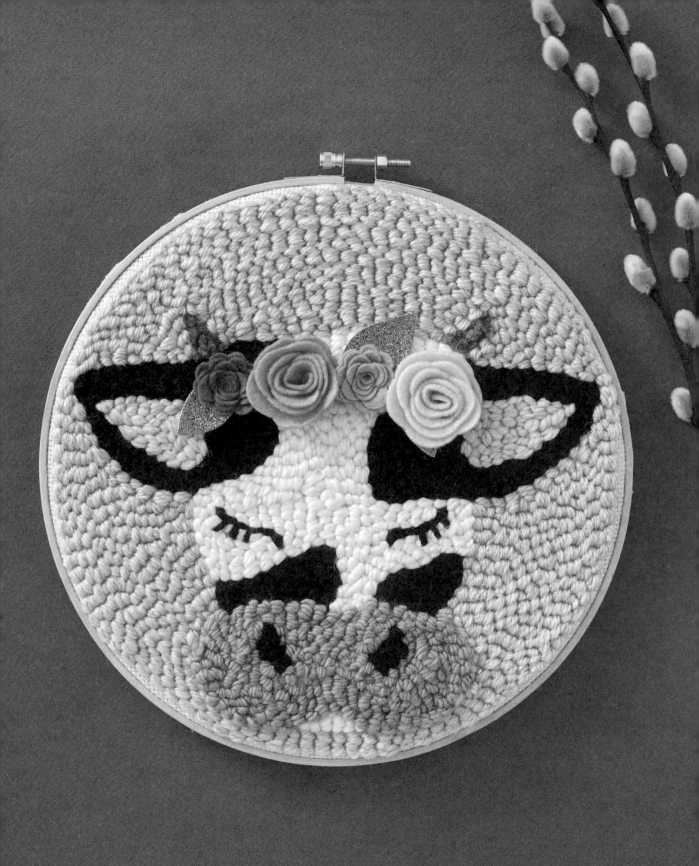

Cow

●●

This little cow is the most charming of the meadows with her crown of flowers. You can change the pattern of the markings—if you want black spots around the eyes, then the eyes should be worked in a lighter shade of yarn.

TOOLS AND MATERIALS

· Monk's cloth fabric 15 x 15in (38 x 38cm)
· Non-slip embroidery hoop 12in (30cm)
· Template 3 (see page 119)
· Marker pen
· Punch needle for super bulky yarn
· Embroidery scissors
· Punch needle for light yarn
· Decorative wooden hoop 10½in (26cm)
· Erasable pen
· Glue gun and glue sticks
· Felt for flowers and leaves (see page 14)

YARN COLORS USED

SUPER BULKY
· Black
· White
· Light pink
· Dark pink
· Brown
· Beige

LIGHT
· Black

STITCHES USED

SEE PAGE 13 FOR STITCH GUIDE
· Flat
· Looped

WORKING IN RELIEF

The shaded areas of the diagram show the parts of the design that should be worked on the back of the canvas. This creates longer loops that may be cut to create additional texture and relief. For instructions on how to transfer the design to both sides of the canvas, see page 10.

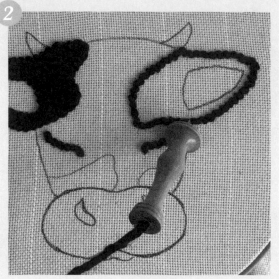

Stretch the canvas over the embroidery hoop (see page 11) and reproduce the design on the front of the canvas (see page 10). Reproduce the elements to be in relief on the back of the canvas (see page 10). Thread the punch needle with black yarn (see page 11).

Insert the needle in the corner of one eye on the front side. On the back side, pull the thread through, leaving a tail of around 1¼in (3cm). Work both eyes, then continue in black yarn to create the spots, starting with the outline and working toward the center.

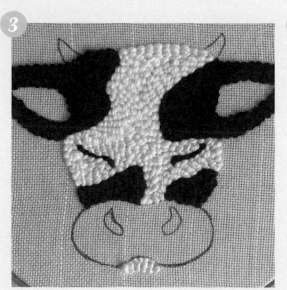

Thread the white yarn and fill the rest of the cow's face and the mouth.

Thread the light pink yarn and fill the ears on the front of the canvas.

5

Turn the hoop over, thread the dark pink yarn, and fill in the muzzle, working from the outside to the inside.

6

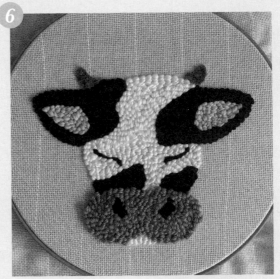

Thread the black yarn and work the nostrils on the back side of the canvas. Thread the light black yarn, turn the hoop over, and add the eyelashes by inserting the needle at the edge of the eye. Finish by threading the brown yarn and adding the horns.

7

Using the inner ring of the decorative hoop, draw a circle around the cow's head with an erasable pen. Thread the beige yarn and fill this circle, working from the outside to the inside. Once finished, remove the canvas from the embroidery hoop and fit it on the decorative hoop (see page 15).

TEMPLATE
4

Panda

●●●●●●●●●●●●●●●●●●●●●●●●●●●●●●●●●●●●●●

This cuddly panda is made using three types of stitches: flat,
looped, and cut. You can work a girl panda by adding eyelashes
and using a different color palette. Our final embroidery has been
embellished with a felt bow tie (see page 14).

TOOLS AND MATERIALS

· Monk's cloth fabric 15 x 15in (38 x 38cm)
· Non-slip embroidery hoop 12in (30cm)
· Template 4 (see page 120)
· Marker pen
· Punch needle for super bulky yarn
· Appliqué or embroidery scissors
· Decorative wooden hoop 10½in (26cm)
· Erasable pen
· Glue gun and glue sticks
· Felt for bow (see page 14)

YARN COLORS USED

SUPER BULKY
· Gray
· Black
· White

STITCHES USED

SEE PAGE 13 FOR STITCH GUIDE
· Flat
· Looped
· Cut

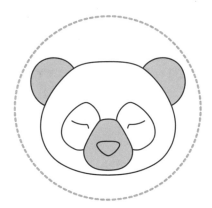

WORKING IN RELIEF
*The shaded areas of the diagram show the parts of
the design that should be worked on the back of the
canvas. This creates longer loops that may be cut to
create additional texture and relief. For instructions on
how to transfer the design to both sides of the canvas,
see page 10.*

Stretch the canvas over the embroidery hoop (see page 11) and reproduce the design on the front of the canvas (see page 10). Reproduce the elements to be in relief on the back of the canvas (see page 10). Thread the punch needle with gray yarn (see page 11).

Insert the needle in the corner of one eye and pull the thread through on the back, leaving a tail of around 1¼in (3cm). Work the first eye. Once finished, leave the needle in the canvas and turn the hoop over. Carefully remove the tip of the needle and cut the thread, leaving about 1¼in (3cm). Repeat for the other eye.

Thread the black yarn and fill in the eye area on the front of the canvas.

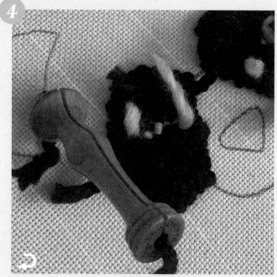

Turn the hoop over and fill in the ears in black. Fill in the nose, also on the back of the canvas.

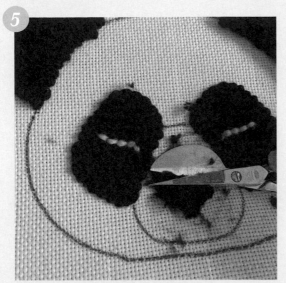

Turn the hoop over to the front and cut the nose loops with the scissors.

Thread the white yarn and fill the muzzle on the back of the canvas, starting with the outline and working from the outside to the inside. When finished, fill the rest of the face in white.

The face of the panda is now finished. Using the inner ring of the decorative hoop, draw a circle around the panda's head with an erasable pen.

Thread the gray yarn and fill in the background of the design, starting with the outline and working from the outside to the inside. Once finished, remove the canvas from the embroidery hoop and fit it on the decorative hoop (see page 15).

Badger

Here is a beautiful badger adorned with a wreath of flowers. We will use three yarn colors and three types of stitches. To add a nice pop of color we chose a background of mustard yellow. The badger's eyes are embroidered in white to contrast with the black.

TOOLS AND MATERIALS

· Monk's cloth fabric 15 x 15in (38 x 38cm)
· Non-slip embroidery hoop 12in (30cm)
· Template 5 (see page 120)
· Marker pen
· Punch needle for super bulky yarn
· Appliqué or embroidery scissors
· Punch needle for light yarn
· Decorative wooden hoop 10½in (26cm)
· Erasable pen
· Glue gun and glue sticks
· Felt for flowers and leaves (see page 14)

YARN COLORS USED

SUPER BULKY
· White
· Black
· Yellow

LIGHT
· White

STITCHES USED

SEE PAGE 13 FOR STITCH GUIDE
· Flat
· Looped
· Cut

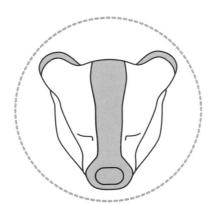

WORKING IN RELIEF

The shaded areas of the diagram show the parts of the design that should be worked on the back of the canvas. This creates longer loops that may be cut to create additional texture and relief. For instructions on how to transfer the design to both sides of the canvas, see page 10.

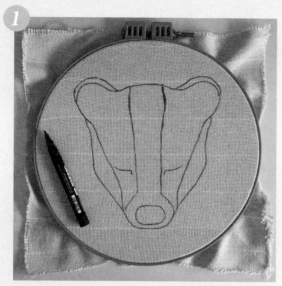

Stretch the canvas over the embroidery hoop (see page 11) and reproduce the design on the front of the canvas (see page 10). Reproduce the elements to be in relief on the back of the canvas (see page 10). Thread the punch needle with white yarn (see page 11).

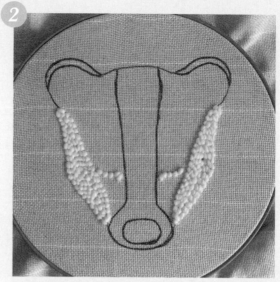

Insert the needle in the corner of one eye and pull the thread through on the back, leaving a tail of around 1¼in (3cm). Work the first eye. Once finished, leave the needle in the canvas and turn the hoop over. Remove the tip of the needle and cut the thread, leaving 1¼in (3cm). Work the other eye and the sides of the face.

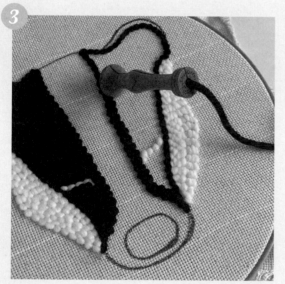

Thread the punch needle with black yarn and fill in the black parts of the face on the front of the canvas.

Turn the hoop over and fill in the nose in black. Turn the hoop over again to the front side and cut the loops using the scissors to create a fluffy effect.

Thread the white yarn, return and fill in the middle of the face and tips of the ears on the back of the canvas.

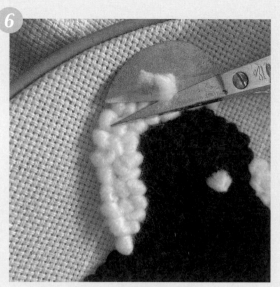

Turn the hoop over to the front side and cut the loops of the ear tips. Thread the light white yarn, and add the eyelashes by inserting the needle at the edge of the eye. Cut the thread on the back and do the same for the other lashes. The badger's face is now complete.

Using the inner ring of the decorative hoop, draw a circle around the badger's head with an erasable pen.

Thread the yellow yarn and fill in the background of the design, starting with the outline and working from the outside to the inside. Once finished, remove the canvas from the embroidery hoop and fit it on the decorative hoop (see page 15).

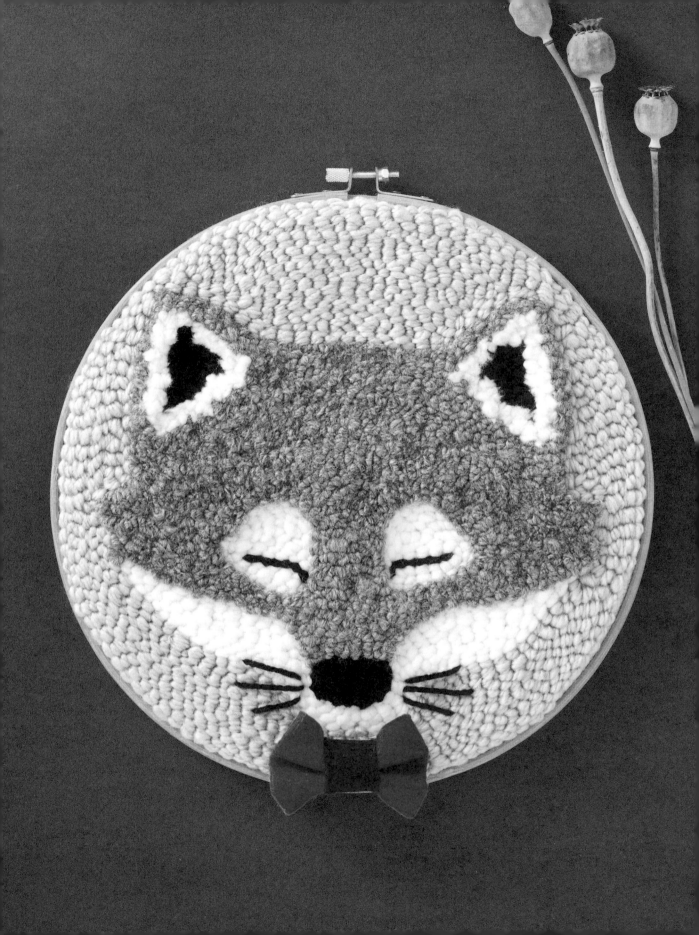

Wolf

This friendly-looking wolf is a world away from the Big Bad Wolf in the fairy tales, with his cute bow tie and soft, snuggly coat that we will create with cut loops. We will use three types of stitches in this design and work on both sides of the canvas.

TOOLS AND MATERIALS

· Monk's cloth fabric 15 x 15in (38 x 38cm)
· Non-slip embroidery hoop 12in (30cm)
· Template 6 (see page 121)
· Marker pen
· Punch needle for super bulky yarn
· Appliqué or embroidery scissors
· Decorative wooden hoop 10½in (26cm)
· Erasable pen
· Punch needle for light yarn
· Glue gun and glue sticks
· Felt for bow (see page 14)

YARN COLORS USED

SUPER BULKY
· Black
· White
· Gray
· Blue

LIGHT
· Black

STITCHES USED

SEE PAGE 13 FOR STITCH GUIDE
· Flat
· Looped
· Cut

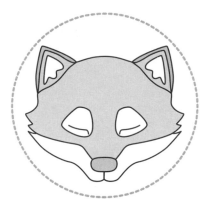

WORKING IN RELIEF

The shaded areas of the diagram show the parts of the design that should be worked on the back of the canvas. This creates longer loops that may be cut to create additional texture and relief. For instructions on how to transfer the design to both sides of the canvas, see page 10.

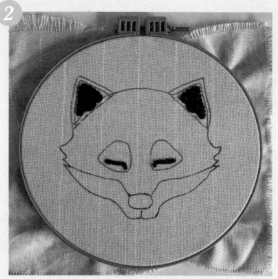

Stretch the canvas over the embroidery hoop (see page 11) and reproduce the design on the front of the canvas (see page 10). Reproduce the elements to be in relief on the back of the canvas (see page 10). Thread the punch needle with black yarn (see page 11).

Insert the needle in the corner of one eye and pull the thread through on the back, leaving a tail of around 1¼in (3cm). Work the first eye. Once finished, leave the needle in the canvas and turn the hoop over. Remove the tip of the needle and cut the thread, leaving about 1¼in (3cm). Work the other eye and insides of the ears.

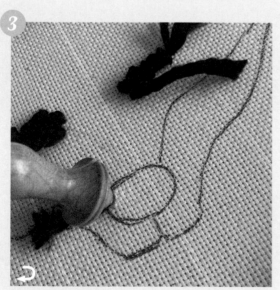

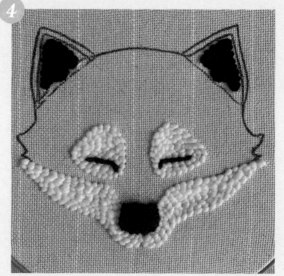

Turn the hoop over to the back and fill the nose in black. Turn the hoop over to the front and cut the nose loops using the scissors.

Thread the white yarn and fill in the eye area and the lower part of the wolf's face on the front of the canvas.

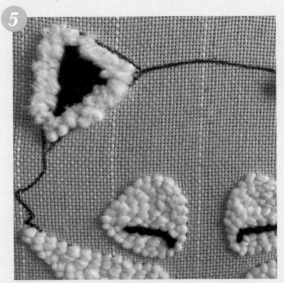

Turn the hoop over to the back and fill in the ears in white. On the front, cut the white ear loops using the scissors.

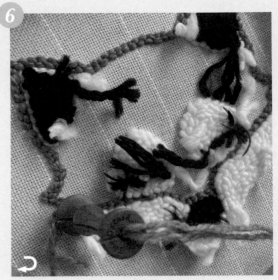

On the back side, fill in the rest of the face in gray yarn, working from the outside to the inside. Once finished, cut the loops to create a furry effect (except for the muzzle to keep the relief). The wolf's face is now complete.

Using the inner ring of the decorative hoop, draw a circle around the wolf's head with an erasable pen. Thread the blue yarn and fill in the background of the design, starting with the outline and working from the outside to the inside.

Thread the light black yarn, and add whiskers by inserting the needle on the front side. Cut the thread that comes out on the back side and repeat for the other whiskers. Once finished, remove the canvas from the embroidery hoop and fit it on the decorative hoop (see page 15).

Cat

●■●

Here is a cute little Angora cat—we will give her a soft coat by cutting the loops. You can change the colors and markings if you would like to create a particular cat. You could also create a boy cat by changing the color scheme and moving the bow to the neck.

TOOLS AND MATERIALS

· Monk's cloth fabric 15 x 15in (38 x 38cm)
· Non-slip embroidery hoop 12in (30cm)
· Transfer 3 from iron-on transfer sheet (see envelope at back of book). Note: the stripes on the cat's head should be reproduced on the back of the canvas only.
· Marker pen
· Punch needle for super bulky yarn
· Appliqué or embroidery scissors
· Decorative wooden hoop 10½in (26cm)
· Erasable pen
· Punch needle for light yarn
· Glue gun and glue sticks
· Felt for bow (see page 14)

YARN COLORS USED

SUPER BULKY

· Black
· Pink
· White
· Beige
· Ecru

LIGHT

· Black

STITCHES USED

SEE PAGE 13 FOR STITCH GUIDE

· Flat
· Cut

WORKING IN RELIEF

The shaded areas of the diagram show the parts of the design that should be worked on the back of the canvas. This creates longer loops that may be cut to create additional texture and relief. For instructions on how to transfer the design to the back of the canvas, see page 10.

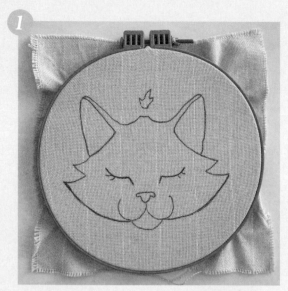

Stretch the canvas over the embroidery hoop (see page 11), then reproduce the design on the front of the canvas using the iron-on transfer sheet (see envelope at back of book). Reproduce the elements to be in relief on the back of the canvas (see page 10). Thread the punch needle with black yarn (see page 11).

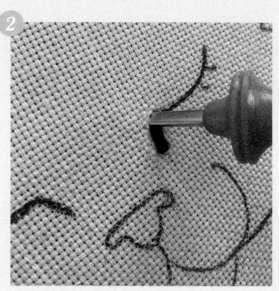

Insert the needle in the corner of one eye and pull the thread through on the back, leaving a tail of around 1¼in (3cm). Work the first eye. Once finished, leave the needle in the canvas and turn the hoop over. Remove the tip of the needle and cut the thread, leaving about 1¼in (3cm). Work the other eye.

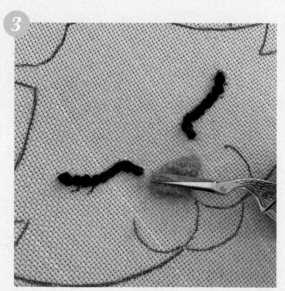

Thread the pink yarn, turn the hoop over to the back, and fill in the nose. Turn the hoop over to the front and cut the nose loops using the scissors.

Thread the white yarn and fill in the eye area on the front of the canvas.

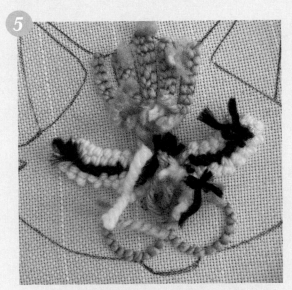

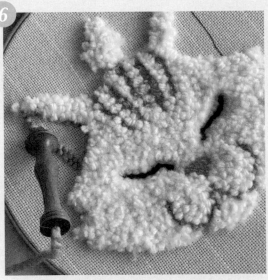

Thread the beige yarn, turn the hoop over to the back, and fill in the stripes and the outline of the muzzle. On the front, cut the loops of the stripes on the head using the scissors.

On the back side, fill in the rest of the face in ecru yarn. Once finished, cut the loops on the front to create a furry effect. Thread the beige yarn and fill the insides of the ears. The cat's face is now complete.

Using the inner ring of the decorative hoop, draw a circle around the cat's head with an erasable pen. Thread the pink yarn and fill in the background of the design, starting with the outline and working from the outside to the inside. Thread the light black yarn and add eyelashes by inserting the needle on the front side. Cut the thread that comes out on the back side and repeat for the other eyelashes and whiskers. Once finished, remove the canvas from the embroidery hoop and fit it on the decorative hoop (see page 15).

Dog

●●●●●●●●●●●●●●●●●●●●●●●●●●●●●●●●●●●●●●

This Cavalier King Charles has the most beautiful long ears. Here we will discover a new stitch: the long cut loop, which involves manually making the loop larger by pulling the thread. We will use this stitch to create the fur of the ears.

TOOLS AND MATERIALS

· Monk's cloth fabric 15 x 15in (38 x 38cm)
· Non-slip embroidery hoop 12in (30cm)
· Template 8 (see page 122)
· Marker pen
· Punch needle for super bulky yarn
· Appliqué or embroidery scissors
· Punch needle for light yarn
· Decorative wooden hoop 10½in (26cm)
· Erasable pen
· Glue gun and glue sticks
· Felt for flowers and leaves (see page 14)

YARN COLORS USED

SUPER BULKY
· Black
· Brown
· White
· Camel
· Gray

LIGHT
· Black

STITCHES USED

SEE PAGE 13 FOR STITCH GUIDE
· Flat
· Looped
· Cut
· Long cut loop

WORKING IN RELIEF

The shaded areas of the diagram show the parts of the design that should be worked on the back of the canvas. This creates longer loops that may be cut to create additional texture and relief. For instructions on how to transfer the design to both sides of the canvas, see page 10.

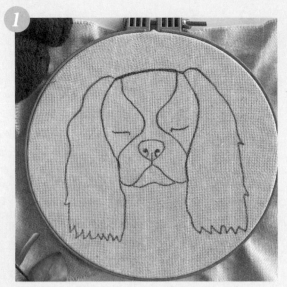

Stretch the canvas over the embroidery hoop (see page 11) and reproduce the design on the front of the canvas (see page 10). Reproduce the elements to be in relief on the back of the canvas (see page 10). Thread the punch needle with black yarn (see page 11).

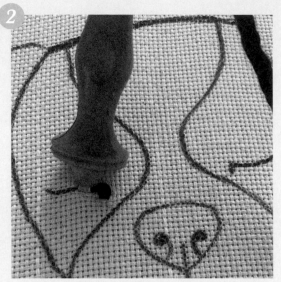

Insert the needle in the corner of one eye and pull the thread through on the back, leaving a tail of around 1¼in (3cm). Work the first eye. Once finished, leave the needle in the canvas and turn the hoop over. Remove the tip of the needle and cut the thread, leaving 1¼in (3cm). Work the other eye and nostrils.

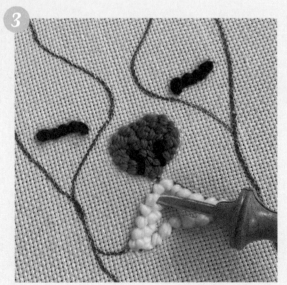

Thread the brown yarn and work the nose on the front of the canvas. Then thread the white yarn and fill in the bottom of the mouth.

Turn the hoop over to the back, and fill in the muzzle and forehead in white. On the front, cut the loops just created using the scissors.

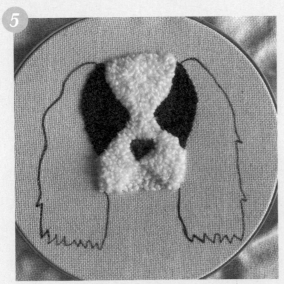

Thread the camel yarn and fill in the sides of the face on the front of the canvas.

Turn the hoop over to the back and fill in the ears in camel. Pull the loops on the front around every three stitches to create longer loops. Start with the outline of each ear and work from the outside to the inside. Turn the hoop over and cut the long loops.

Thread the light black yarn and work the mouth. The dog's face is now complete. Using the inner ring of the decorative hoop, draw a circle around the dog's head with an erasable pen.

Thread the gray yarn and fill in the background of the design, starting with the outline and working from the outside to the inside. Once finished, remove the canvas from the embroidery hoop and fit it on the decorative hoop (see page 15).

TEMPLATE
9

Otter

●●

This little otter appears to be taking a nap while floating on the surface of the water. Her nose is made of cut loops, the muzzle is looped stitch, and the rest of the design is worked in flat stitch. The long whiskers are added when the embroidery is complete.

TOOLS AND MATERIALS

· Monk's cloth fabric 15 x 15in (38 x 38cm)
· Non-slip embroidery hoop 12in (30cm)
· Template 9 (see page 122)
· Marker pen
· Punch needle for super bulky yarn
· Appliqué or embroidery scissors
· Decorative wooden hoop 10½in (26cm)
· Erasable pen
· Punch needle for light yarn
· Glue gun and glue sticks
· Felt for flowers and leaves (see page 14)

YARN COLORS USED

SUPER BULKY
· Black
· Ecru
· Brown
· Light blue

LIGHT
· Black

STITCHES USED

SEE PAGE 13 FOR STITCH GUIDE
· Flat
· Looped
· Cut

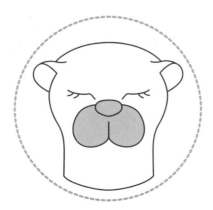

WORKING IN RELIEF

The shaded areas of the diagram show the parts of the design that should be worked on the back of the canvas. This creates longer loops that may be cut to create additional texture and relief. For instructions on how to transfer the design to both sides of the canvas, see page 10.

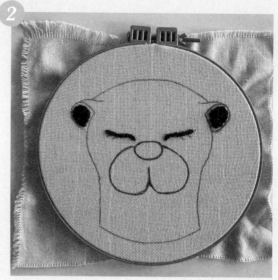

Stretch the canvas over the embroidery hoop (see page 11) and reproduce the design on the front of the canvas (see page 10). Reproduce the elements to be in relief on the back of the canvas (see page 10). Thread the punch needle with black yarn (see page 11).

Insert the needle in the corner of one eye and pull the thread through on the back, leaving a tail of around 1¼in (3cm). Work the first eye. Once finished, leave the needle in the canvas and turn the hoop over. Remove the tip of the needle and cut the thread, leaving 1¼in (3cm). Work the other eye and the insides of the ears.

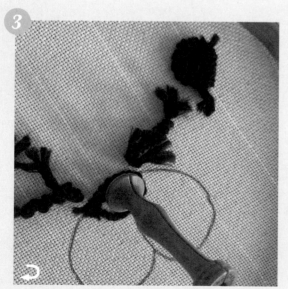

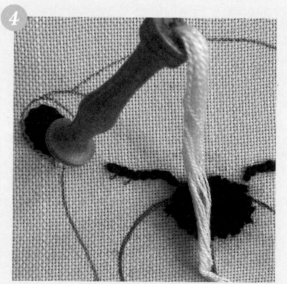

Turn the hoop over to the back and fill the nose in black. Turn the hoop over to the front and cut the nose loops using the scissors.

Thread the ecru yarn and fill in the outline of the ears on the front of the canvas.

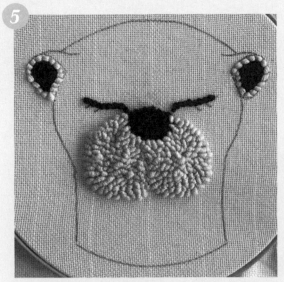

Turn the hoop over to the back and fill in the muzzle with ecru.

Thread the brown yarn and fill in the rest of the face on the front of the canvas, working from the outside to the inside. The otter's face is now complete.

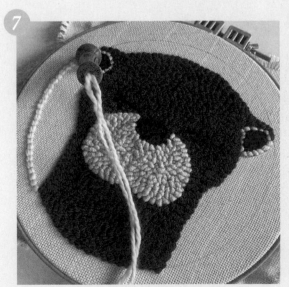

Using the inner ring of the decorative hoop, draw a circle around the otter's head with an erasable pen. Thread the light blue yarn and fill in the background of the design, starting with the outline and working from the outside to the inside.

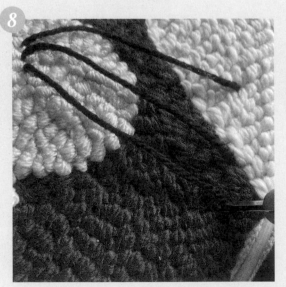

Thread the light black yarn and add whiskers by inserting the needle on the front side. Cut the thread on the back and repeat for the other whiskers. Add a small dot of glue to the end of each whisker to fix in place. Once finished, remove the canvas from the embroidery hoop and fit it on the decorative hoop (see page 15).

Doe

This pretty pastel doe is made using three punch needle stitches, the trickiest being the loop stitches. We have embellished the final embroidery with little felt flowers and sparkly leaves in dusky pinks and golds.

TOOLS AND MATERIALS
· Monk's cloth fabric 15 x 15in (38 x 38cm)
· Non-slip embroidery hoop 12in (30cm)
· Transfer 4 from iron-on transfer sheet (see envelope at back of book)
· Marker pen
· Punch needle for super bulky yarn
· Appliqué or embroidery scissors
· Punch needle for light yarn
· Decorative wooden hoop 10½in (26cm)
· Erasable pen
· Glue gun and glue sticks
· Felt for flowers and leaves (see page 14)

YARN COLORS USED
SUPER BULKY
· Black
· White
· Brown
· Ecru
· Pink

LIGHT
· Black

STITCHES USED
SEE PAGE 13 FOR STITCH GUIDE
· Flat
· Looped
· Cut

WORKING IN RELIEF
The shaded areas of the diagram show the parts of the design that should be worked on the back of the canvas. This creates longer loops that may be cut to create additional texture and relief. For instructions on how to transfer the design to the back of the canvas, see page 10.

1

Stretch the canvas over the embroidery hoop (see page 11), then reproduce the design on the front of the canvas using the iron-on transfer sheet (see envelope at back of book). Reproduce the elements to be in relief on the back of the canvas (see page 10). Thread the punch needle with black yarn (see page 11).

2

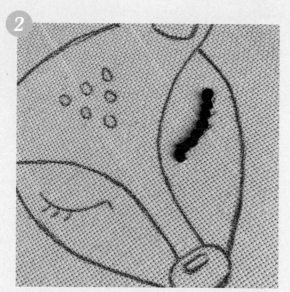

Insert the needle in the corner of one eye and pull the thread through on the back, leaving a tail of around 1¼in (3cm). Work the first eye. Once finished, leave the needle in the canvas and turn the hoop over. Remove the tip of the needle and cut the thread, leaving 1¼in (3cm). Work the other eye.

3

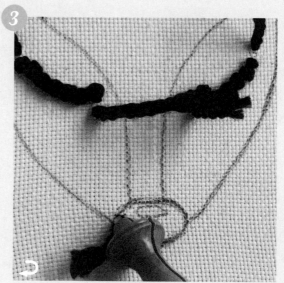

Turn the hoop over to the back and fill the nose in black.

Turn the hoop over to the front and use the scissors to cut the nose loops to create a fluffy effect.

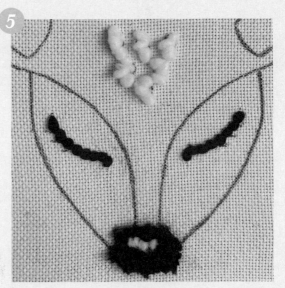

Thread the white yarn, turn the hoop over to the back, and add the white spots on the nose and head.

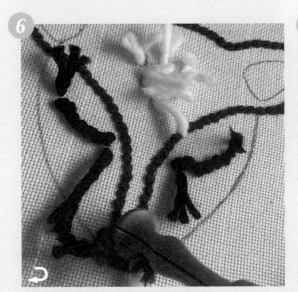

Thread the brown yarn and fill in the top of the face on the back of the canvas, working from the outside to the inside.

Thread the ecru yarn and fill in the rest of the face plus the insides of the ears on the front side of the canvas.

8

Thread the light black yarn and add eyelashes by inserting the needle on the front side of the canvas.

9

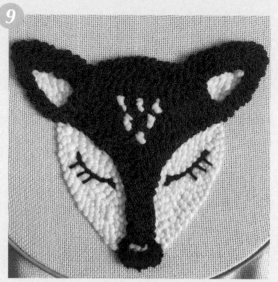

Cut the thread that comes out on the back side and repeat for the other eyelashes. The doe's face is complete.

10

Using the inner ring of the decorative hoop, draw a circle around the doe's head with an erasable pen.

Thread the pink yarn and fill in the background of the design, starting with the outline.

Work in circles from the outside to the inside, until you have filled in the pink background. Once finished, remove the canvas from the embroidery hoop and fit it on the decorative hoop (see page 15).

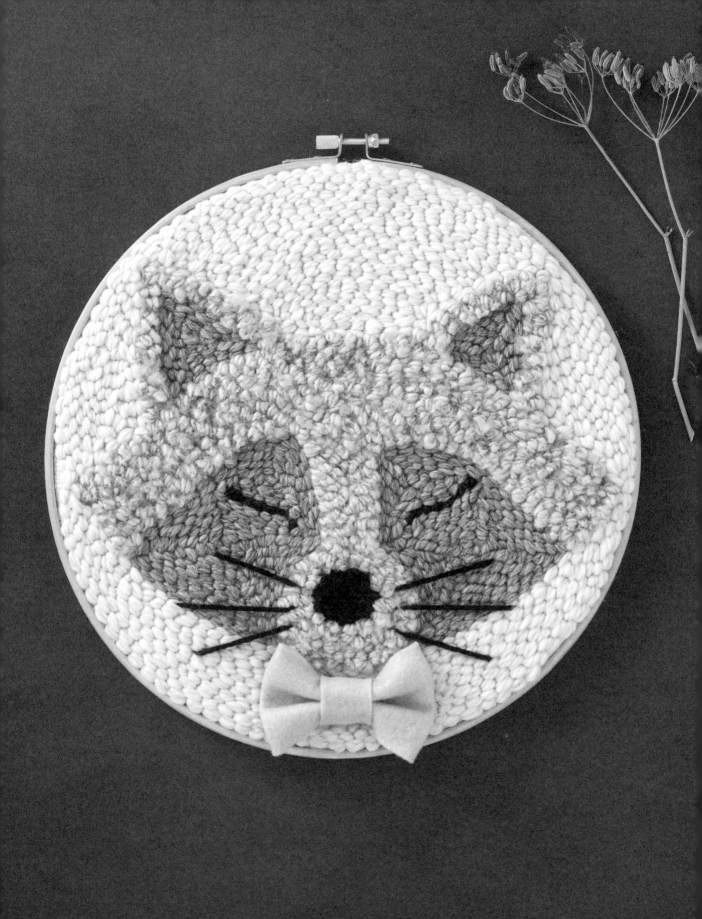

TRANSFER 5

Raccoon

●●●●●●●●●●●●●●●●●●●●●●●●●●●●●●●●●●●●●●●

Here is a handsome gray raccoon with very soft fur that we will create by cutting the loops of the light gray yarn. The whiskers are added once the embroidery is complete. You could create a girl raccoon by adding eyelashes and moving the bow to the head.

TOOLS AND MATERIALS

· Monk's cloth fabric 15 x 15in (38 x 38cm)
· Non-slip embroidery hoop 12in (30cm)
· Transfer 5 from iron-on transfer sheet (see envelope at back of book)
· Marker pen
· Punch needle for super bulky yarn
· Appliqué or embroidery scissors
· Decorative wooden hoop 10½in (26cm)
· Erasable pen
· Punch needle for light yarn
· Glue gun and glue sticks
· Felt for bow (see page 14)

YARN COLORS USED

SUPER BULKY
· Black
· Light gray
· Dark gray
· Light green

LIGHT
· Black

STITCHES USED

SEE PAGE 13 FOR STITCH GUIDE
· Flat
· Looped
· Cut

WORKING IN RELIEF

The shaded areas of the diagram show the parts of the design that should be worked on the back of the canvas. This creates longer loops that may be cut to create additional texture and relief. For instructions on how to transfer the design to the back of the canvas, see page 10.

Stretch the canvas over the embroidery hoop (see page 11), then reproduce the design on the front of the canvas using the iron-on transfer sheet (see envelope at back of book). Reproduce the elements to be in relief on the back of the canvas (see page 10). Thread the punch needle with black yarn (see page 11).

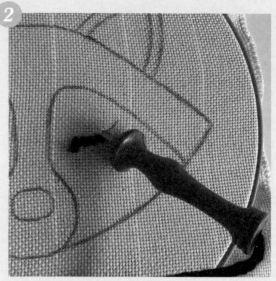

Insert the needle in the corner of one eye and pull the thread through on the back, leaving a tail of around 1¼in (3cm). Work the first eye. Once finished, leave the needle in the canvas and turn the hoop over. Remove the tip of the needle and cut the thread, leaving about 1¼in (3cm). Work the other eye.

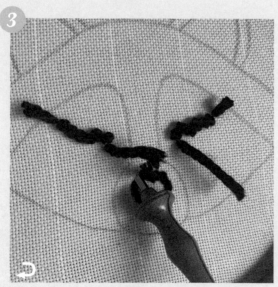

Turn the hoop over to the back side and fill the nose in black.

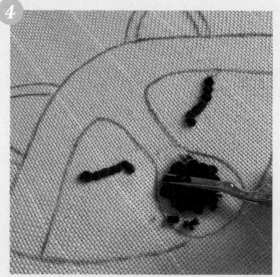

Turn the hoop over to the front and cut the nose loops using the scissors.

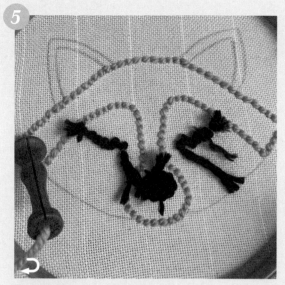

Thread the light gray yarn, and on the back side, fill in the top of the face, around the nose, and the outside of the ears.

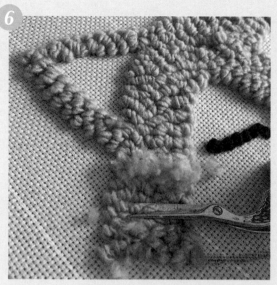

Turn the hoop over to the front and cut the light gray loops to create a fluffy effect.

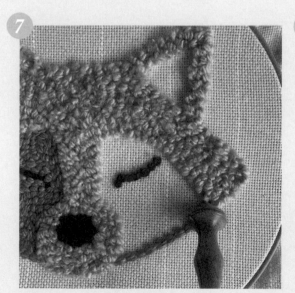

Thread the dark gray yarn and fill in the rest of the face on the front of the canvas.

Fill in the insides of the ears with the same yarn on the front of the canvas.

The raccoon's face is complete.

Using the inner ring of the decorative hoop, draw a circle around the raccoon's head with an erasable pen.

Thread the light green yarn and fill in the background of the design, starting with the outline and working from the outside to the inside.

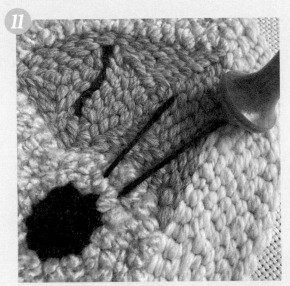

Thread the light black yarn and add whiskers by inserting the needle on the front side.

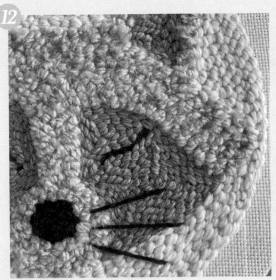

Cut the thread that comes out on the back side and repeat for the other whiskers.

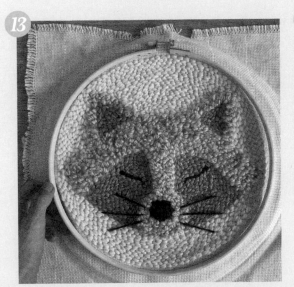

Once finished, remove the canvas from the embroidery hoop and fit it on the decorative hoop (see page 15).

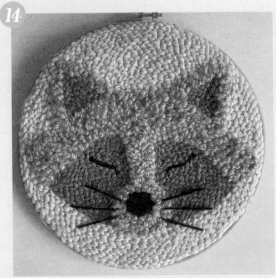

The raccoon is ready to be hung.

Fox

This cute punch needle fox is far more cuddly than the sly foxes in the fairy tales. The cut loops of the orange stitches on his face make his fur beautifully soft and strokable. We added a neutral background to contrast with his striking coat.

TOOLS AND MATERIALS

- Monk's cloth fabric 15 x 15in (38 x 38cm)
- Non-slip embroidery hoop 12in (30cm)
- Transfer 6 from iron-on transfer sheet (see envelope at back of book)
- Marker pen
- Punch needle for super bulky yarn
- Appliqué or embroidery scissors
- Decorative wooden hoop 10½in (26cm)
- Erasable pen
- Punch needle for light yarn
- Glue gun and glue sticks
- Felt for bow (see page 14)

YARN COLORS USED

SUPER BULKY
- Black
- White
- Orange
- Gray

LIGHT
- Black

STITCHES USED

SEE PAGE 13 FOR STITCH GUIDE
- Flat
- Looped
- Cut

WORKING IN RELIEF

The shaded areas of the diagram show the parts of the design that should be worked on the back of the canvas. This creates longer loops that may be cut to create additional texture and relief. For instructions on how to transfer the design to the back of the canvas, see page 10.

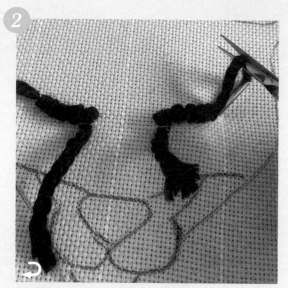

Stretch the canvas over the embroidery hoop (see page 11), then reproduce the design on the front of the canvas using the iron-on transfer sheet (see envelope at back of book). Reproduce the elements to be in relief on the back of the canvas (see page 10). Thread the punch needle with black yarn (see page 11).

Insert the needle in the corner of one eye and pull the thread through on the back, leaving a tail of around 1¼in (3cm). Work the first eye. Once finished, leave the needle in the canvas and turn the hoop over. Remove the tip of the needle and cut the thread (see above), leaving about 1¼in (3cm). Work the other eye.

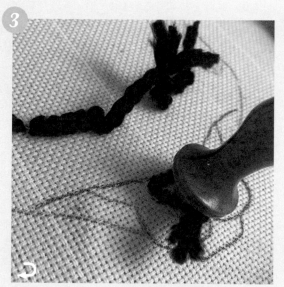

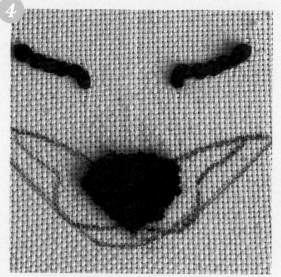

Turn the hoop over to the back and fill the nose in black.

Turn the hoop over to the front and cut the nose loops using the scissors to create a fluffy effect.

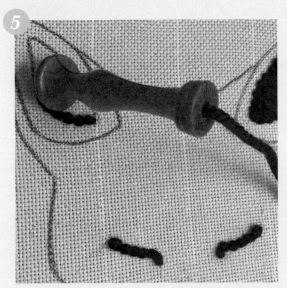

On the front side of the canvas, fill in the insides of the ears with the black yarn.

Thread the white yarn, turn the hoop over to the back, and fill in the muzzle and the outsides of the ears.

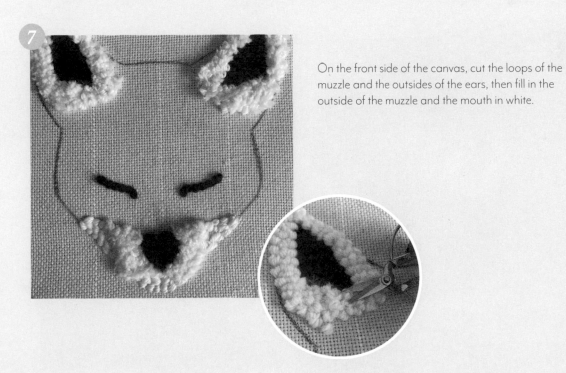

On the front side of the canvas, cut the loops of the muzzle and the outsides of the ears, then fill in the outside of the muzzle and the mouth in white.

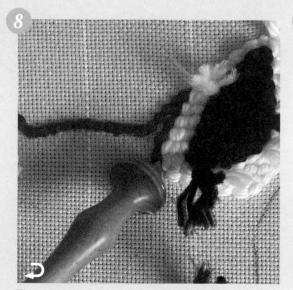

Thread the orange yarn and punch all the way around the eyes twice on the front side of the canvas. Turn the canvas over and fill the rest of the face, working from the outside to the inside.

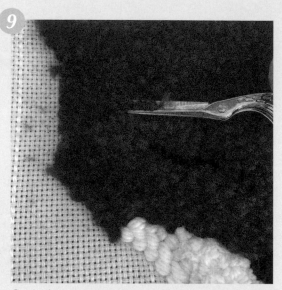

On the front side, cut the loops of the stitches that you just worked on the back side. You could leave these stitches uncut, if you prefer.

The fox's face is complete.

10 Using the inner ring of the decorative hoop, draw a circle around the fox's head with an erasable pen.

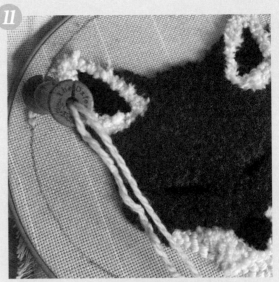

11 Thread the gray yarn and fill in the background of the design, starting with the outline and working from the outside to the inside.

12 Thread the light black yarn and add whiskers by inserting the needle on the front side. Cut the thread that comes out on the back side and repeat for the other whiskers.

13 Once finished, remove the canvas from the embroidery hoop and fit it on the decorative hoop (see page 15).

Red Panda

This adorable red panda is worked mostly on the back of the canvas in order to create the loops that will then be cut in certain places. This technique creates relief and makes the panda stand out from the fabric.

TOOLS AND MATERIALS

· Monk's cloth fabric 15 x 15in (38 x 38cm)
· Non-slip embroidery hoop 12in (30cm)
· Template 11 (see page 124)
· Marker pen
· Punch needle for super bulky yarn
· Appliqué or embroidery scissors
· Decorative wooden hoop 10½in (26cm)
· Erasable pen
· Punch needle for light yarn
· Glue gun and glue sticks

YARN COLORS USED

SUPER BULKY
· Black
· White
· Red
· Beige

LIGHT
· Black

STITCHES USED

SEE PAGE 13 FOR STITCH GUIDE
· Flat
· Looped
· Cut

WORKING IN RELIEF

The shaded areas of the diagram show the parts of the design that should be worked on the back of the canvas. This creates longer loops that may be cut to create additional texture and relief. For instructions on how to transfer the design to both sides of the canvas, see page 10.

Stretch the canvas over the embroidery hoop (see page 11) and reproduce the design on the front of the canvas (see page 10). Reproduce the elements to be in relief on the back of the canvas (see page 10). Thread the punch needle with black yarn (see page 11).

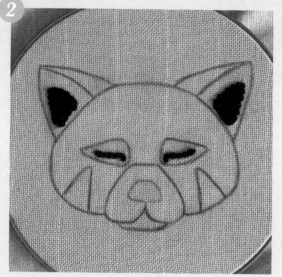

Insert the needle in the corner of one eye and pull the thread through on the back, leaving a tail of around 1¼in (3cm). Work the first eye. Once finished, leave the needle in the canvas and turn the hoop over. Remove the tip of the needle and cut the thread, leaving about 1¼in (3cm). Work the other eye and insides of the ears.

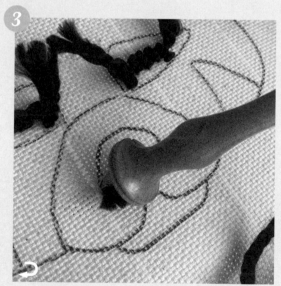

Turn the hoop over to the back and fill the nose in black.

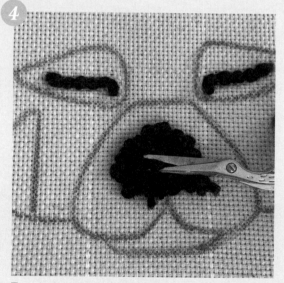

Turn the hoop over to the front and cut the nose loops using the scissors to create a fluffy effect.

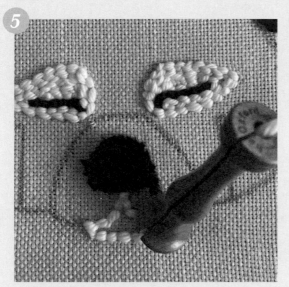

Thread the white yarn and fill in the eye area and the mouth on the front of the canvas.

Turn the hoop over to the back and fill in the muzzle and the cheeks in white.

On the front, cut the loops of the cheeks using the scissors.

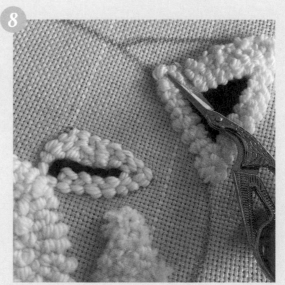

Fill in the white edges of the ears on the back of the canvas, then cut the loops on the front.

Thread the red yarn, turn over to the back side of the canvas, and fill in the head, working from the outside to the inside.

Fill in the tops of the ears in red on the back side of the canvas. The red panda's face is complete.

Using the inner ring of the decorative hoop, draw a circle around the red panda's head with an erasable pen. Thread the beige yarn and fill in the background of the design, starting with the outline and working from the outside to the inside.

Thread the light black yarn and add whiskers by inserting the needle on the front side. Cut the thread that comes out on the back side and repeat for the other whiskers.

Once finished, remove the canvas from the embroidery hoop and fit it on the decorative hoop (see page 15).

TEMPLATE
12

Horse

•••

This sweet horse has a beautifully strokable mane, which is created using the long cut loop. We will highlight her muzzle in relief and the rest of her face will be flat. You can add a colored background to coordinate or contrast with her fur and floral headdress.

TOOLS AND MATERIALS

- Monk's cloth fabric 15 x 15in (38 x 38cm)
- Non-slip embroidery hoop 12in (30cm)
- Template 12 (see page 125)
- Marker pen
- Punch needle for super bulky yarn
- Appliqué or embroidery scissors
- Comb
- Punch needle for light yarn
- Decorative wooden hoop 10½in (26cm)
- Erasable pen
- Glue gun and glue sticks
- Felt for flowers and leaves (see page 14)

YARN COLORS USED

SUPER BULKY

- Black
- White
- Brown
- Beige
- Purple

LIGHT

- Black

STITCHES USED

SEE PAGE 13 FOR STITCH GUIDE

- Flat
- Looped
- Cut
- Long cut loop

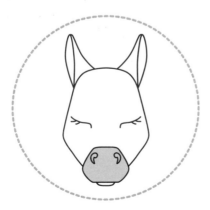

WORKING IN RELIEF

The shaded areas of the diagram show the parts of the design that should be worked on the back of the canvas. This creates longer loops that may be cut to create additional texture and relief. For instructions on how to transfer the design to both sides of the canvas, see page 10.

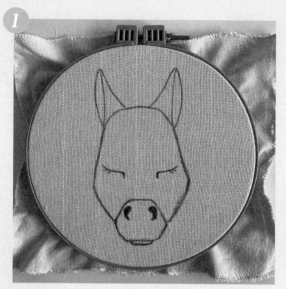

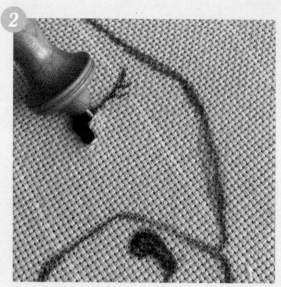

Stretch the canvas over the embroidery hoop (see page 11) and reproduce the design on the front of the canvas (see page 10). Reproduce the elements to be in relief on the back of the canvas (see page 10). Thread the punch needle with black yarn (see page 11).

Insert the needle in the corner of one eye and pull the thread through on the back, leaving a tail of around 1¼in (3cm). Work the first eye. Once finished, leave the needle in the canvas and turn the hoop over. Remove the tip of the needle and cut the thread, leaving about 1¼in (3cm). Work the other eye.

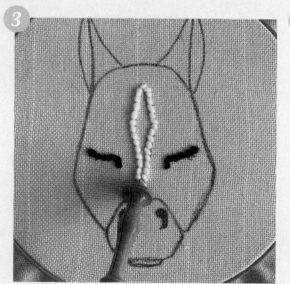

Thread the white yarn and fill in the white part of the head on the front of the canvas.

Thread the brown yarn and fill in the face on the front, working from the outside to the inside.

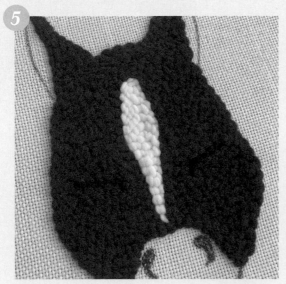

Fill in the outsides of the ears in brown on the front of the canvas.

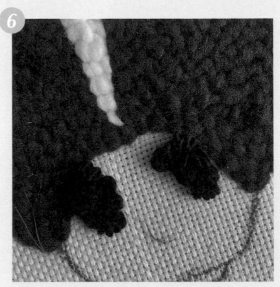

Thread the black yarn, turn the hoop over to the back, and fill in the nostrils.

Thread the beige yarn, stay on the back side of the canvas, and fill in the muzzle.

Return to the front side and fill the mouth in beige.

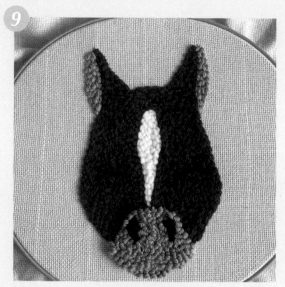

Fill the insides of the ears in beige on the front of the canvas. The horse's face is complete.

To work the forelock, thread the black yarn and punch across the top of the head on the back, gently pulling the thread of each stitch on the front to create a long loop. Create three rows of loops above the head.

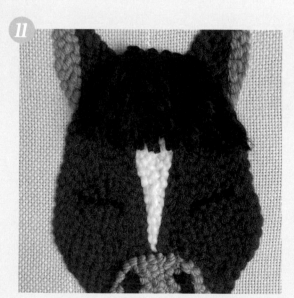

Cut the long loops on the front and comb them gently.

To work the mane, proceed in the same way to create three rows of long loops at the side of the head.

Cut the loops on the front and comb them gently.

Thread the light black yarn and add eyelashes by inserting the needle on the front side. Cut the thread that comes out on the back side and repeat for the other eyelashes.

Using the inner ring of the decorative hoop, draw a circle around the horse's head with an erasable pen. Thread the purple yarn and fill in the background of the design, starting with the outline and working from the outside to the inside.

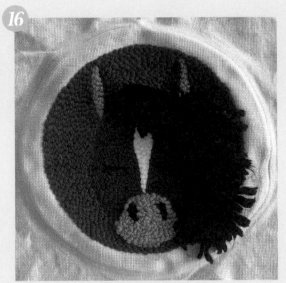

Once finished, remove the canvas from the embroidery hoop and fit it on the decorative hoop (see page 15).

Llama

●●●●●●●●●●●●●●●●●●●●●●●●●●●●●●●●●●●

Here is a pretty soft llama wearing a pastel pink floral headdress, with a pop of color in the background. You could create a boy version by adding a bow tie (see page 14) and leaving out the eyelashes.

TOOLS AND MATERIALS

· Monk's cloth fabric 15 x 15in (38 x 38cm)
· Non-slip embroidery hoop 12in (30cm)
· Transfer 7 from iron-on transfer sheet (see envelope at back of book)
· Marker pen
· Punch needle for super bulky yarn
· Appliqué or embroidery scissors
· Punch needle for light yarn
· Decorative wooden hoop 10½in (26cm)
· Erasable pen
· Glue gun and glue sticks
· Felt for flowers and leaves (see page 14)

YARN COLORS USED

SUPER BULKY

· Black
· Light brown
· Ecru
· Yellow

LIGHT

· Black

STITCHES USED

SEE PAGE 13 FOR STITCH GUIDE

· Flat
· Looped
· Cut

WORKING IN RELIEF

The shaded areas of the diagram show the parts of the design that should be worked on the back of the canvas. This creates longer loops that may be cut to create additional texture and relief. For instructions on how to transfer the design to the back of the canvas, see page 10.

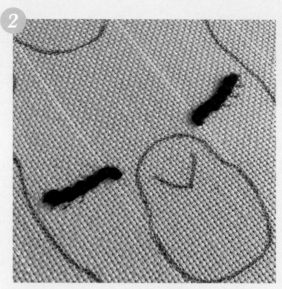

1

Stretch the canvas over the embroidery hoop (see page 11), then reproduce the design on the front of the canvas using the iron-on transfer sheet (see envelope at back of book). Reproduce the elements to be in relief on the back of the canvas (see page 10). Thread the punch needle with black yarn (see page 11).

2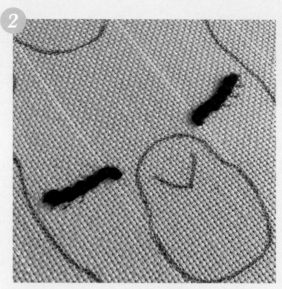

Insert the needle in the corner of one eye and pull the thread through on the back, leaving a tail of around 1¼in (3cm). Work the first eye. Once finished, leave the needle in the canvas and turn the hoop over. Remove the tip of the needle and cut the thread, leaving about 1¼in (3cm). Work the other eye.

3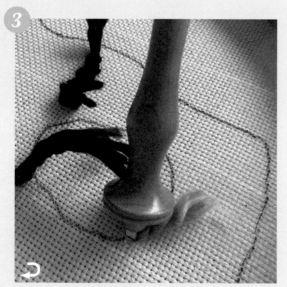

Thread the light brown yarn, turn the hoop over to the back, and work the llama's muzzle.

4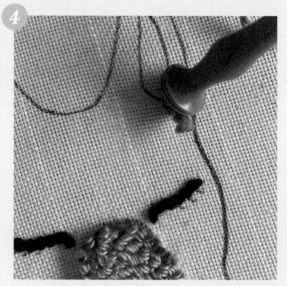

Return to the front side of the canvas and fill the insides of the ears in light brown.

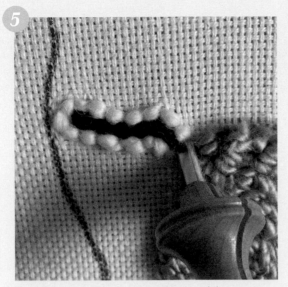

Thread the ecru yarn and punch around the eyes on the front of the canvas.

Turn the hoop over to the back and fill in the rest of the face in ecru, working from the outside to the inside.

Cut the ecru loops with the scissors on the front of the canvas.

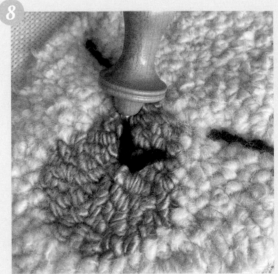

Thread the light black yarn and add the nostrils by inserting the needle on the front of the canvas.

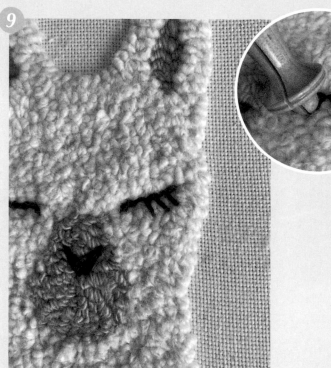

9

10

Add the eyelashes by inserting the needle on the front side of the canvas. Cut the thread that comes out on the back side and repeat for the other eyelashes. The llama's face is now complete.

11

Using the inner ring of the decorative hoop, draw a circle around the llama's head with an erasable pen.

12

Thread the yellow yarn and fill in the background of the design, starting with the outline.

Work in circles from the outside to the inside, until you have filled in the yellow background.

Once finished, remove the canvas from the embroidery hoop and fit it on the decorative hoop (see page 15).

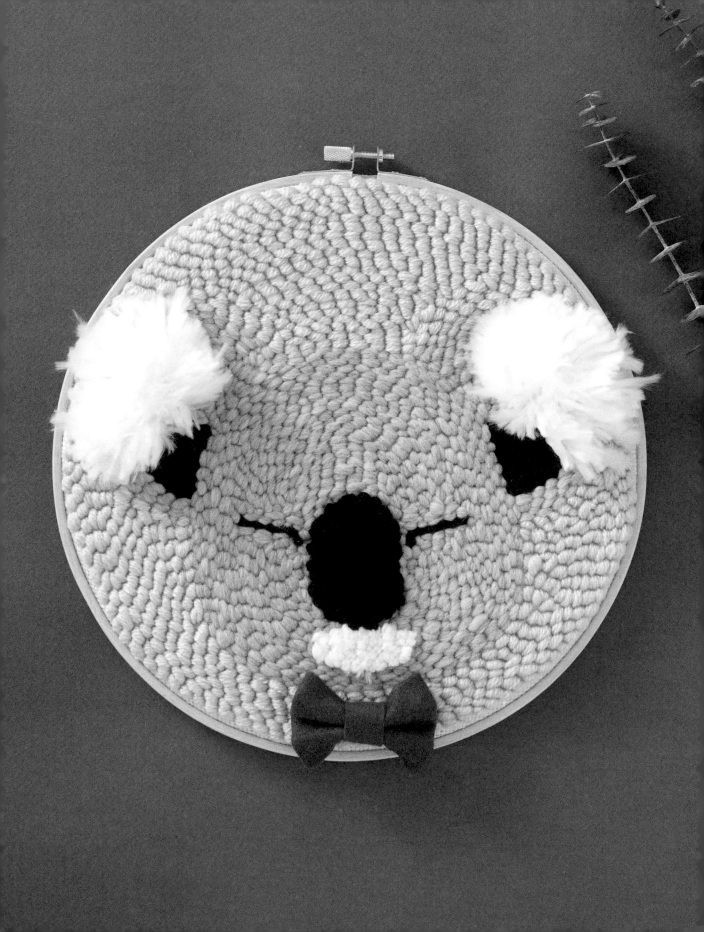

Koala

Here is a sweet koala with fabulous fluffy ears that are great fun to work. This project features four different stitches: the flat stitch for the face, the loops for the nose, the cut loops for the mouth, and the long cut loops for the inside of the ears.

TOOLS AND MATERIALS
· Monk's cloth fabric 15 x 15in (38 x 38cm)
· Non-slip embroidery hoop 12in (30cm)
· Transfer 8 from iron-on transfer sheet (see envelope at back of book)
· Marker pen
· Punch needle for super bulky yarn
· Appliqué or embroidery scissors
· Comb
· Decorative wooden hoop 10½in (26cm)
· Erasable pen
· Glue gun and glue sticks
· Felt for bow (see page 14)

YARN COLORS USED
SUPER BULKY
· Black
· Gray
· White
· Beige

STITCHES USED
SEE PAGE 13 FOR STITCH GUIDE
· Flat
· Looped
· Cut
· Long cut loop

WORKING IN RELIEF
The shaded areas of the diagram show the parts of the design that should be worked on the back of the canvas. This creates longer loops that may be cut to create additional texture and relief. For instructions on how to transfer the design to the back of the canvas, see page 10.

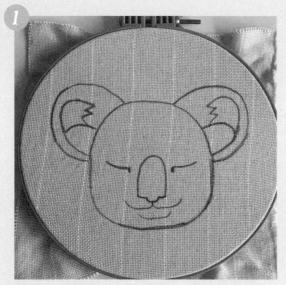

Stretch the canvas over the embroidery hoop (see page 11), then reproduce the design on the front of the canvas using the iron-on transfer sheet (see envelope at back of book). Reproduce the elements to be in relief on the back of the canvas (see page 10). Thread the punch needle with black yarn (see page 11).

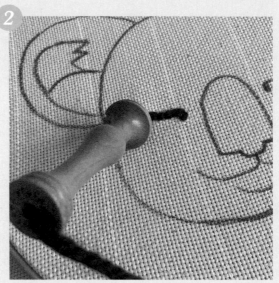

Insert the needle in the corner of one eye and pull the thread through on the back, leaving a tail of around 1¼in (3cm). Work the first eye. Once finished, leave the needle in the canvas and turn the hoop over. Remove the tip of the needle and cut the thread, leaving about 1¼in (3cm). Work the other eye.

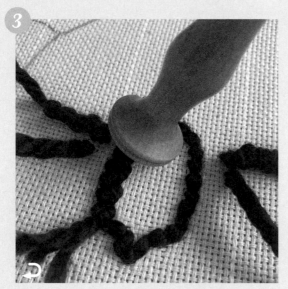

Turn the hoop over to the back and fill the nose in black.

Return to the front side of the canvas and fill in the insides of the ears in black.

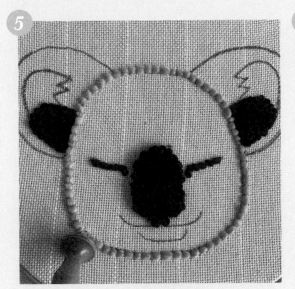

Thread the gray yarn and fill in the head on the front side of the canvas, working from the outside to the inside.

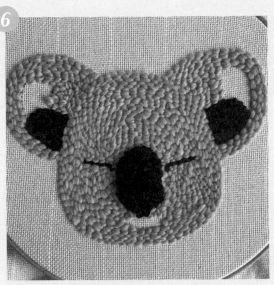

Stay on the front side of the canvas and fill in the ears in gray.

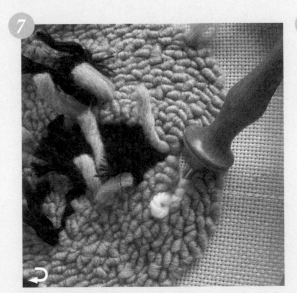

Thread the white yarn, turn the hoop over to the back, and work the mouth.

Cut the white loops of the mouth on the front side of the canvas.

9

Return to the back side and work the remaining part of the insides of the ears in white. Pull the thread of each stitch gently on the front to create longer loops.

10

Cut the long loops with the scissors to create fringes.

11

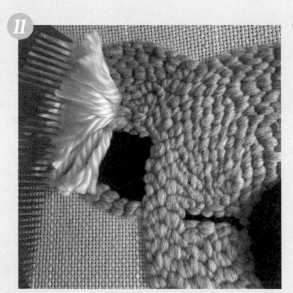

Comb the fringes to separate the strands of yarn and create a fluffy effect.

12

Trim the fringes to create a pompom shape. The koala's face is complete.

Using the inner ring of the decorative hoop, draw a circle around the koala's head with an erasable pen.

Thread the beige yarn and fill in the background of the design, starting with the outline.

Work in circles from the outside to the inside, until you have filled in the beige background.

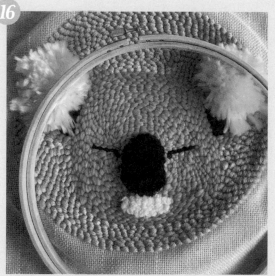

Once finished, remove the canvas from the embroidery hoop and fit it on the decorative hoop (see page 15).

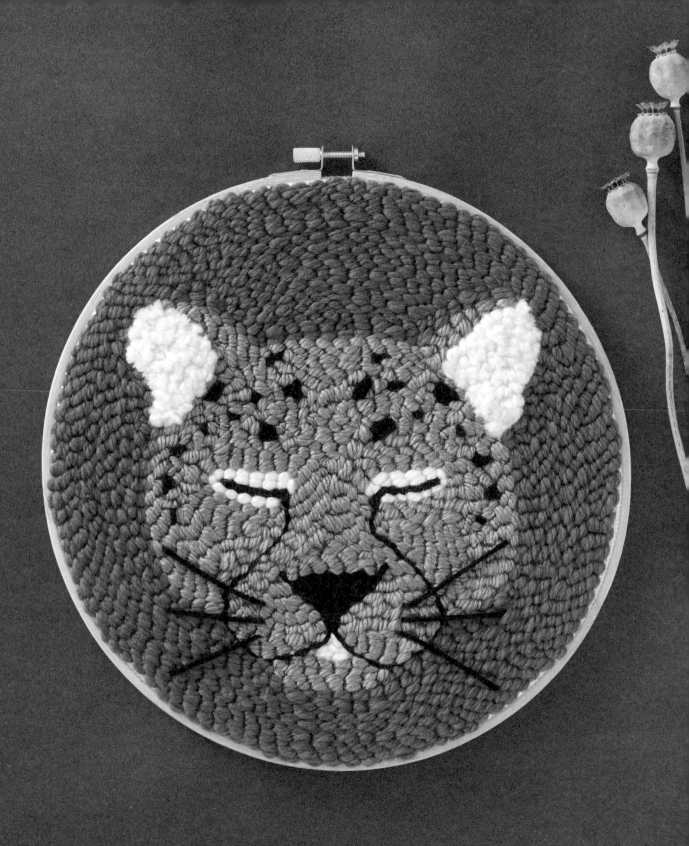

Leopard

••

This majestic leopard is created using only two types of stitches but contains a little more detail than the other projects, in the fur markings and the outline of the muzzle.

TOOLS AND MATERIALS

· Monk's cloth fabric 15 x 15in (38 x 38cm)
· Non-slip embroidery hoop 12in (30cm)
· Transfer 9 from iron-on transfer sheet (see envelope at back of book)
· Marker pen
· Punch needle for super bulky yarn
· Appliqué or embroidery scissors
· Punch needle for light yarn
· Decorative wooden hoop 10½in (26cm)
· Erasable pen
· Glue gun and glue sticks

YARN COLORS USED

SUPER BULKY
· Black
· Ecru
· Beige
· Green

LIGHT
· Black

STITCHES USED

SEE PAGE 13 FOR STITCH GUIDE
· Flat
· Cut

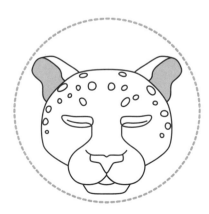

WORKING IN RELIEF

The shaded areas of the diagram show the parts of the design that should be worked on the back of the canvas. This creates longer loops that may be cut to create additional texture and relief. For instructions on how to transfer the design to the back of the canvas, see page 10.

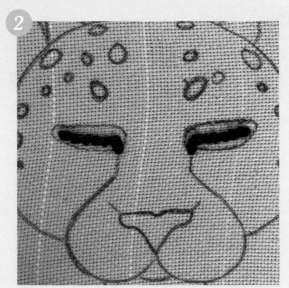

1

Stretch the canvas over the embroidery hoop (see page 11), then reproduce the design on the front of the canvas using the iron-on transfer sheet (see envelope at back of book). Reproduce the elements to be in relief on the back of the canvas (see page 10). Thread the punch needle with black yarn (see page 11).

2

Insert the needle in the corner of one eye and pull the thread through on the back, leaving a tail of around 1¼in (3cm). Work the first eye. Once finished, leave the needle in the canvas and turn the hoop over. Remove the tip of the needle and cut the thread, leaving about 1¼in (3cm). Work the other eye.

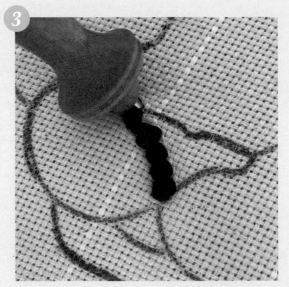

3

Fill in the nose in black on the front of the canvas.

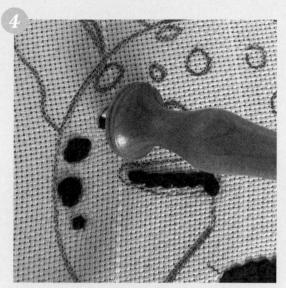

4 Remaining on the front, work all the leopard's spots in black.

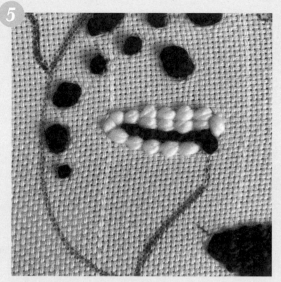

5 Thread the ecru yarn and fill around the eyes and the bottom of the mouth on the front of the canvas.

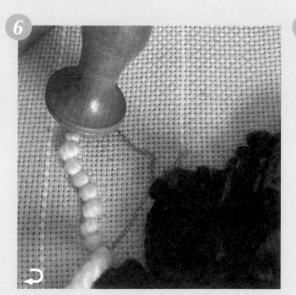

6 Turn the hoop over to the back and fill the insides of the ears in ecru.

7 Cut the loops of the ears on the front using the scissors.

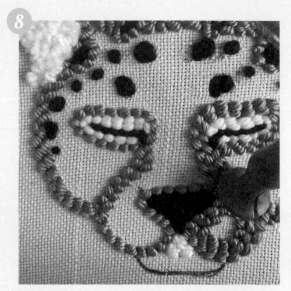

Thread the beige yarn and fill in the rest of the face on the front of the canvas, working from the outside to the inside.

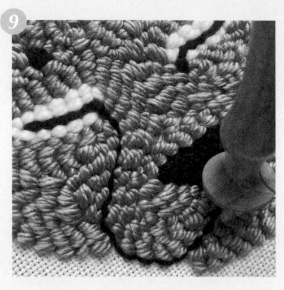

Thread the light black yarn and work the outline of the muzzle on the front of the canvas.

Work one diagonal stitch in light black yarn at either side of the nose as shown. The leopard's face is now complete.

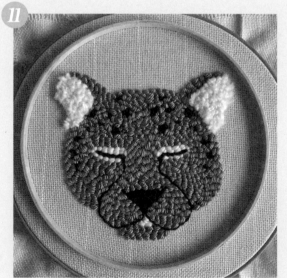

Using the inner ring of the decorative hoop, draw a circle around the leopard's head with an erasable pen.

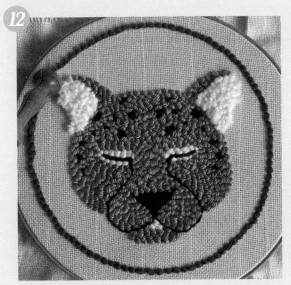

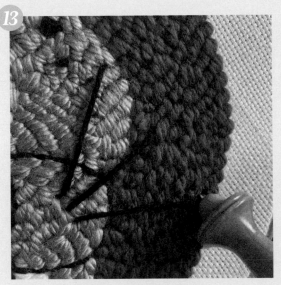

Thread the green yarn and fill in the background of the design, starting with the outline. Work in circles from the outside to the inside, until you have filled in the green background.

Thread the light black yarn and add whiskers by inserting the needle on the front side. Cut the thread that comes out on the back side and repeat for the other whiskers. Once finished, remove the canvas from the embroidery hoop and fit it on the decorative hoop (see page 15).

TRANSFER 10

Sloth

●●●●●●●●●●●●●●●●●●●●●●●●●●●●●●●●●●●●

This happily snoozing sloth is the only project in the book with hands as the sloth's long claws are so distinctive, helping him to hang upside down in the trees. The face is worked in the flat stitch and the rest in loops or cut loops.

TOOLS AND MATERIALS

· Monk's cloth fabric 15 x 15in (38 x 38cm)
· Non-slip embroidery hoop 12in (30cm)
· Transfer 10 from iron-on transfer sheet (see envelope at back of book)
· Marker pen
· Punch needle for super bulky yarn
· Appliqué or embroidery scissors
· Decorative wooden hoop 10½in (26cm)
· Erasable pen
· Glue gun and glue sticks
· Felt for leaves (see page 14)

YARN COLORS USED

SUPER BULKY

· Black
· Dark brown
· Ecru
· Light brown
· Green

STITCHES USED

SEE PAGE 13 FOR STITCH GUIDE

· Flat
· Looped
· Cut

WORKING IN RELIEF

The shaded areas of the diagram show the parts of the design that should be worked on the back of the canvas. This creates longer loops that may be cut to create additional texture and relief. For instructions on how to transfer the design to the back of the canvas, see page 10.

Stretch the canvas over the embroidery hoop (see page 11), then reproduce the design on the front of the canvas using the iron-on transfer sheet (see envelope at back of book). Reproduce the elements to be in relief on the back of the canvas (see page 10). Thread the punch needle with black yarn (see page 11).

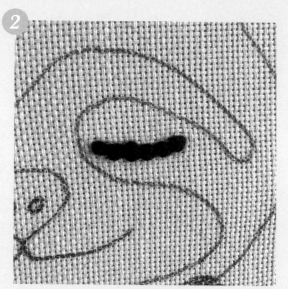

Insert the needle in the corner of one eye and pull the thread through on the back, leaving a tail of around 1¼in (3cm). Work the first eye. Once finished, leave the needle in the canvas and turn the hoop over. Remove the tip of the needle and cut the thread, leaving about 1¼in (3cm). Work the other eye.

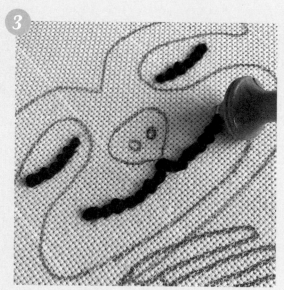

Work the mouth in black on the front of the canvas.

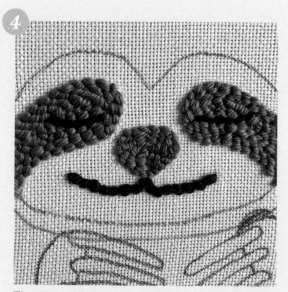

Thread the dark brown yarn and, on the front of the canvas, fill around the eyes and the nose.

Thread the black yarn and add the nostrils on the front of the canvas.

Remaining on the front, thread the ecru yarn and work the face, working from the outside to the inside.

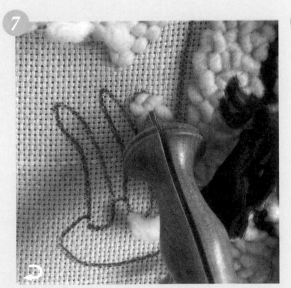

Turn the hoop over to the back and fill in the claws in ecru.

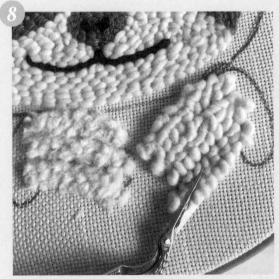

Cut the loops of the claws on the front of the canvas with the scissors.

Thread the light brown yarn and work the rest of the sloth's head on the back of the canvas, working from the outside to the inside.

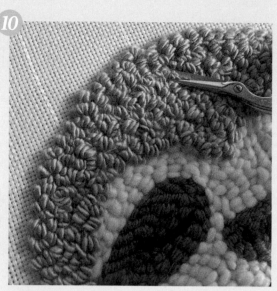

Turn the hoop over and cut the light brown loops of the head with the scissors.

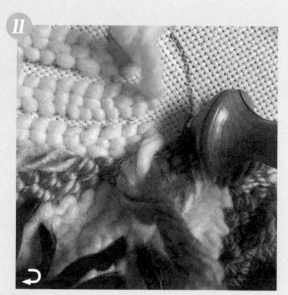

Thread the dark brown yarn and work the paws on the back of the canvas.

The sloth's face is complete. Using the inner ring of the decorative hoop, draw a circle around the sloth's head with an erasable pen.

Thread the green yarn and fill in the background of the design, starting with the outline. Work in circles from the outside to the inside, until you have filled in the green background.

Once finished, remove the canvas from the embroidery hoop and fit it on the decorative hoop (see page 15).

TRANSFER 9

Lion

●●

This regal lion is the most time-consuming yet satisfying project in the book because of his superb mane made from long cut loops. Once finished, it covers the whole of the decorative hoop and gives him a real presence, like the king of the savanna.

TOOLS AND MATERIALS

· Monk's cloth fabric 15 x 15in (38 x 38cm)
· Non-slip embroidery hoop 12in (30cm)
· Transfer 9 from iron-on transfer sheet (see envelope at back of book). Note: this is a dual-purpose transfer. For the lion, omit the leopard's spots.
· Marker pen
· Punch needle for super bulky yarn
· Appliqué or embroidery scissors
· Comb
· Punch needle for light yarn
· Decorative wooden hoop 10½in (26cm)
· Glue gun and glue sticks

YARN COLORS USED

SUPER BULKY
· Black
· Beige
· Ecru
· Brown

LIGHT
· Black

STITCHES USED

SEE PAGE 13 FOR STITCH GUIDE
· Flat
· Looped
· Cut
· Long cut loop

WORKING IN RELIEF

The shaded areas of the diagram show the parts of the design that should be worked on the back of the canvas. This creates longer loops that may be cut to create additional texture and relief. For instructions on how to transfer the design to the back of the canvas, see page 10.

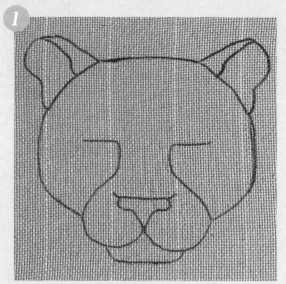

1

Stretch the canvas over the embroidery hoop (see page 11), then reproduce the design on the front of the canvas using the iron-on transfer sheet (see envelope at back of book). Reproduce the elements to be in relief on the back of the canvas (see page 10). Thread the punch needle with black yarn (see page 11).

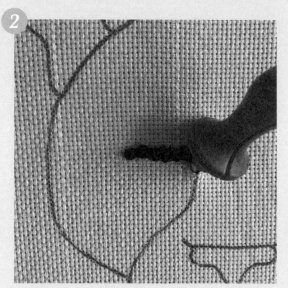

2

Insert the needle in the corner of one eye and pull the thread through on the back, leaving a tail of around 1¼in (3cm). Work the first eye. Once finished, leave the needle in the canvas and turn the hoop over. Remove the tip of the needle and cut the thread, leaving 1¼in (3cm). Work the other eye.

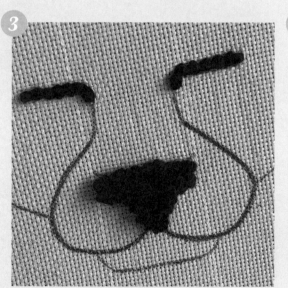

3

Turn the hoop over to the back and fill the nose in black.

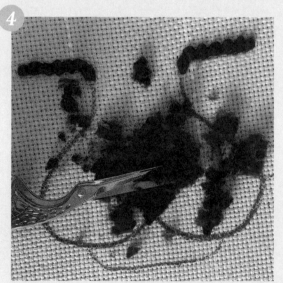

4

Turn the hoop over to the front and cut the nose loops using the scissors to create a fluffy effect.

5

Thread the beige yarn, turn the hoop over to the back, and fill in the muzzle.

6

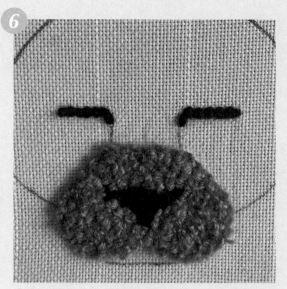

On the front, cut the loops of the muzzle using the scissors.

7

Fill in the mouth in beige on the front of the canvas.

8

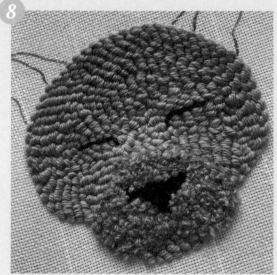

Fill in the rest of the face in beige on the front of the canvas, working from the outside to the inside.

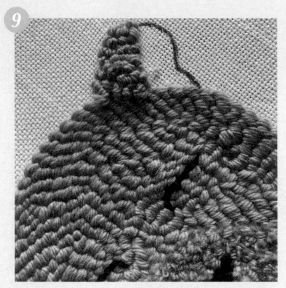

Turn the hoop over to the back and fill in the tops of the ears in beige.

Thread the ecru yarn and fill in the insides of the ears on the back of the canvas.

Cut the ecru loops with the scissors on the front of the canvas.

Thread the brown yarn and work the outline of the muzzle on the front of the canvas.

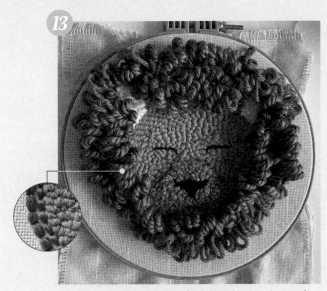

Work around the outline of the head on the back of the canvas, gently pulling the thread of each stitch on the front to create a long loop. Create two rounds of loops around the head (shown on the back of the canvas in the insert).

Cut the long loops on the front to create fringes and comb them gently.

Thread the light black yarn and add whiskers by inserting the needle on the front side. Cut the thread that comes out on the back side and repeat for the other whiskers.

Once finished, remove the canvas from the embroidery hoop and fit it on the decorative hoop (see page 15).

Templates

On these pages you will find templates for all the designs in the book. Start by enlarging the required template by 50 percent on a photocopier and then follow the instructions on page 10 to transfer the design to your canvas. The templates marked with an iron icon can also be found at full size on the iron-on transfer sheets in the envelope at the back of the book. See opposite for instructions on how to use the iron-on transfers, then follow the instructions on page 10 to transfer the design to the back of your canvas.

Polar Bear see page 18

TRANSFER 1

Rabbit see page 22

TEMPLATE 1

USING THE IRON-ON TRANSFERS
To apply an iron-on transfer, start by cutting around the motif, leaving some spare paper all around. Place the transfer, ink-side down, in position on the fabric. Heat the iron to a medium setting suitable for your fabric. Place the hottest part of the iron—the center—over the transfer area and hold for about ten seconds. Do not move the iron, since this may blur the transferred lines. If necessary, lift and replace the iron until all areas of the template have been covered.

Giraffe see page 26
TRANSFER 2

Cow see page 30
TEMPLATE 3

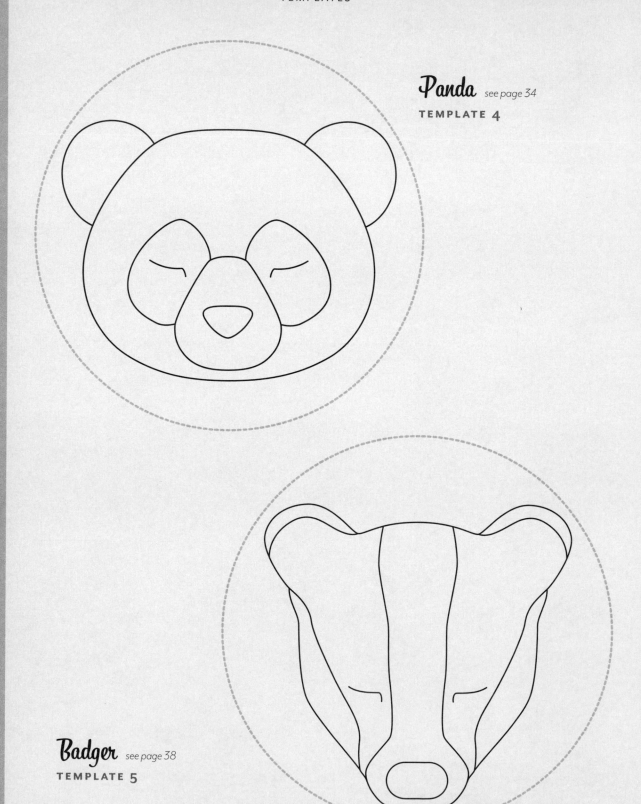

Panda see page 34

TEMPLATE 4

Badger see page 38

TEMPLATE 5

Wolf see page 42
TEMPLATE 6

Giraffe see page 26
TRANSFER 2

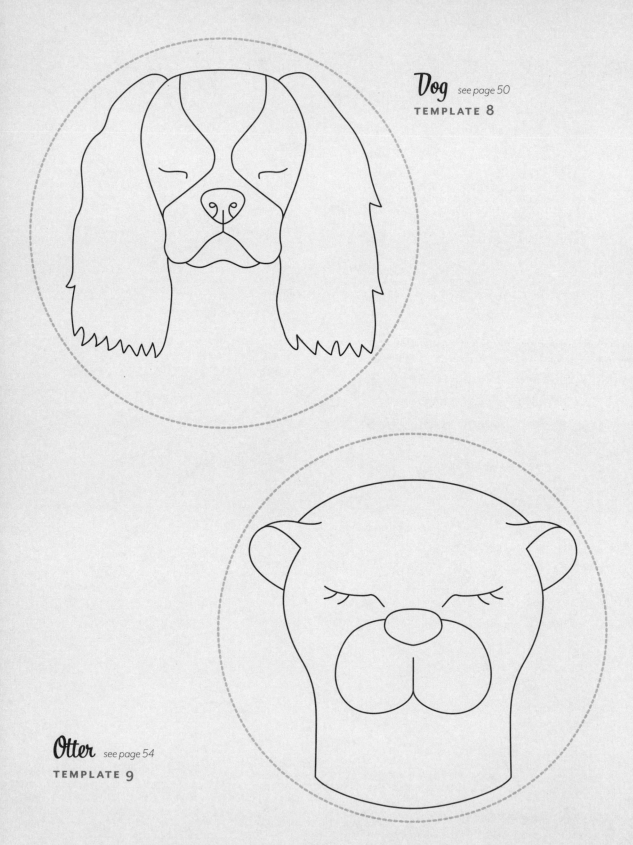

Dog *see page 50*
TEMPLATE 8

Otter *see page 54*
TEMPLATE 9

Doe see page 58

TRANSFER 4

Raccoon see page 64

TRANSFER 5

Fox see page 70

TRANSFER 6

Red Panda see page 76

TEMPLATE 11

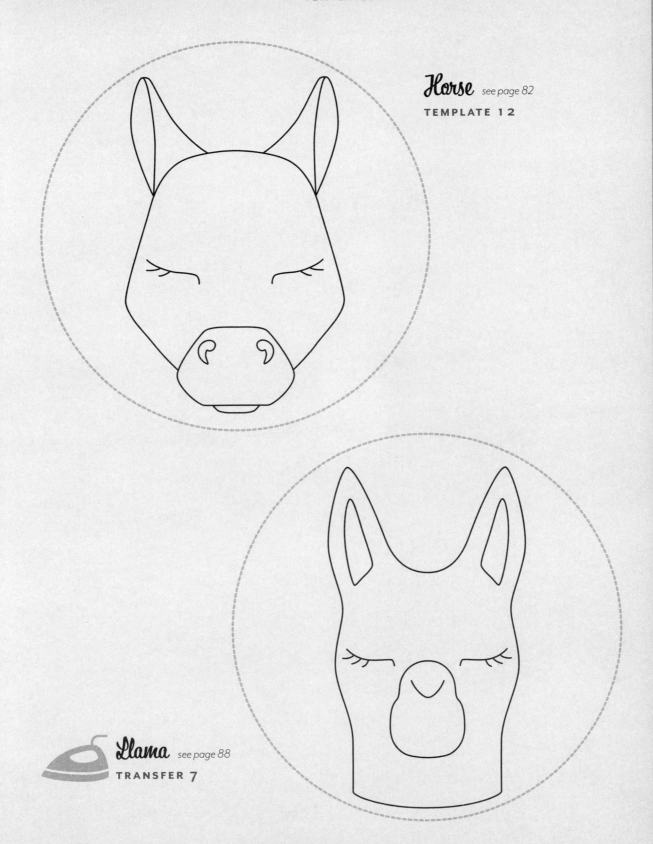

Horse see page 82

TEMPLATE 12

Llama see page 88

TRANSFER 7

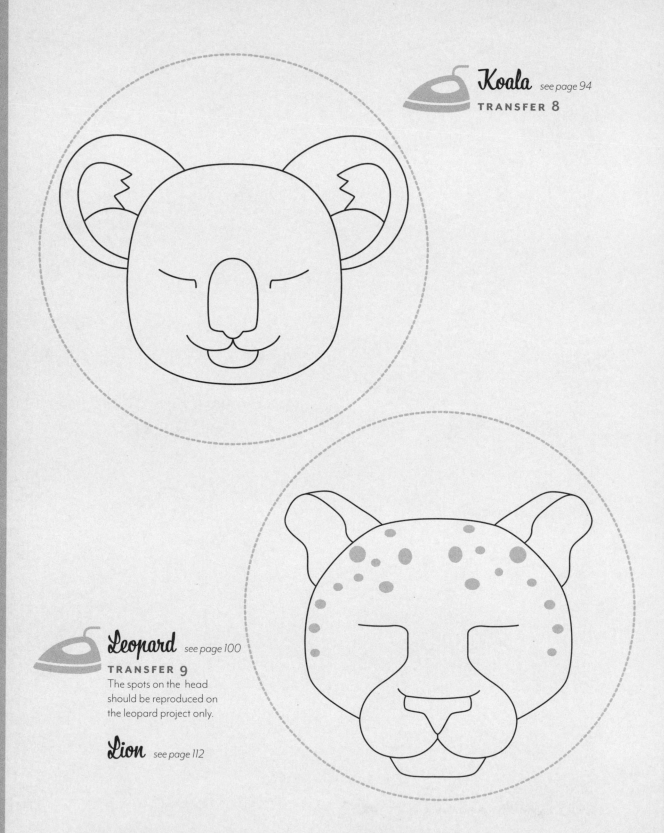

Koala see page 94

TRANSFER 8

Leopard see page 100

TRANSFER 9

The spots on the head should be reproduced on the leopard project only.

Lion see page 112

Sloth see page 106

TRANSFER 10

Embellishments templates

Below you will find templates for the bow, flower, and leaf embellishments used in the designs. Start by enlarging the required template by 50 percent on a photocopier and then follow the instructions on page 14 to create the embellishment.

Bow see page 14

Flower see page 14

Leaf see page 14

Leaf see page 14

Index

Credits

Page 6: photo © Manon Isorce

Page 14: Flower pattern was inspired by the DIY Felt Rolled Flower on theyellowbirdhouse.com